What's gamed in court;
is forced onto the streets.

What's proven in PASS;
is proven on the streets.

The Law Doctor

THE
LAW
DOCTOR

With higher standards

By Licensed Author
Aaron W. Wemple

Clean Law Union

www.CleanLawUnion.com

(Licensed Authors are scientifically established martyrs for truth.)

What's gamed in court;
is forced onto the streets.
4
What's proven in PASS;
is proven on the streets.

The Law Doctor

Published by Clean Law Union

International Standard Book Number: 978-0-9851567-9-4

International Standard eBook Number: 978-0-9851567-7-0

1. Law 2. Engineering 3. Social Science 4. Christian 5. Government

Printed in the United States of America
with Constitutional jurisprudence.

For information:
Clean Law Union
www.CleanLawUnion.com

What's gamed in court;
is forced onto the streets.

What's proven in PASS;
is proven on the streets.

Healing the cause of intellectual cancers:

Drowning the spirits of love;
Was no safe way to lead;
Teaching the world to fly again;
Now there's a safe place to be.

Dedicated to enlightenment.

The Law Doctor

Contents

HIGHER STANDARDS

HEALING SOLUTIONS

INCUBATING CURES

THINKING ANEW

What's gamed in court;
is forced onto the streets.

What's proven in PASS;
is proven on the streets.

The Law Doctor

What's gamed in court;
is forced onto the streets.   10   *What's proven in PASS;*
is proven on the streets.

Bearing witness to light;

Especially where it opposes light;

Especially where it opposes light on several different levels;

Especially where it opposes light on several different levels and many different fronts;

Especially where opposing light on several different levels and on many different fronts grows by both figurative "law" and by literal Leverage;

And especially where bearing witness to the light hurts by both figurative "laws" and/or literal Leverages;

But especially in the United States of America.

What's gamed in court;
is forced onto the streets.

What's proven in PASS;
is proven on the streets.

The Law Doctor

Introduction

Wow! Where do I begin?

Could there really be so much bully-ism going on this world?

Could there really not be?!

Could we just ignore it all and just "*make*" it magically go away?

Nope. Absolutely not today.

This book is about the dynamics that inherently build up from unlevel relations. Relations as old as mankind. But this time in scientific standards.

This book is a deep look into bullies and the victims of bullies.

The victim in this book tried for years to get the bullies to wake up, to stop insulting and assaulting their own victim, and to change their ways. But the worse that the bullies got, the worse the bullies got.

"So, I'll at least slow them down," the victim began to cry." For what else can a little guy do?

But when the most superficial bullies of all had the bullies back, then the little guy was lost, left all on his own. He was fabricated to be without a clue.

So superficial were these biggest bullies that they themselves were literally detached from reality. They simply hovered around like big monstrous genies.

And they forced their own victims to be detached from reality too. Just so that they'd be easier to victimize. So really, nobody even had a clue.

So what's a bullied little compulsively victimized victim to do?

Stay stuck there without a clue?!

Legally, our highest bullies, the ones who can and will do the most damage to us, are off of limits to us. And in what world does that make any sense?

I'll tell you in what world that makes sense. In a bullies world this makes perfect sense!

You see, when the little guy gets fed-up with all of the antics and the "*antidotes*" that he can take, then why not enlighten them all from a severed place? At least they can't touch me there.

What else can one do when bullies who are detached from reality and behind closed doors victimize you? Just lie down and die without a clue?

So the little guy decided that there must be one more thing that he can do. Maybe he can shine through and enlighten others who had no clue?

What's gamed in court;
is forced onto the streets.   20   *What's proven in PASS;*
is proven on the streets.

The more that he thought about it the more that he understood that this was not about solving problems after they have become a major, catastrophic, national epidemic. But more than that it was about resurrection. And even more than that it was about the salvation of all of man-kind.

After all, what's a little guy to do when the leaders of many nations steps all over him like he was meant to pick up their broken little pieces a million times infinity? And then try to put himself back together again too without any glue?

I'll tell you what he does. He starts making glue. He plans something new. And then he solves their problems too. And then he tries to enlighten you.

So he thought, "why divide when we can unite?!"

There, that should do.

After all, isn't that what we are meant to do?

It should not be the little people who are liable for bigger people's mistakes. Some jobs can and will simply neglect us to death.

At worse, it should be the big jobs liable to the little people when mistakes are exposed. This would prevent murder-ization from neglect.

And now with science by his side,
that little person presents to you
something old, something new, something
borrowed & something blue.

But most of all something uniting.
Something uniting and enlightening to
stick us back together again like glue.

Something uniting and something new
for both me and for you.

There, that's what we should do!

News flash bullies!

I bet that you didn't know science
rules too?!

HIGHER STANDARDS

What's gamed in court;
is forced onto the streets.   23   *What's proven in PASS;*
is proven on the streets.

The Law Doctor

1. Lower than fishing food

"The Constitution only gives people the right to pursue happiness. You have to catch it yourself."
- *Benjamin Franklin*

No truer words where ever spoken.

In Florida it's illegal to feed the sharks. It's illegal to feed the sharks because it makes them aggressive.
Why is it legal to civilize animals <u>and</u> legal to uncivilize humans?

Let's find out what's eating us shall we?

In Illinois I'm promoting that State legislators make it illegal to feed judicial sharks. Or psychological warriors, as they are known. They're already known

What's gamed in court;
is forced onto the streets.   25   *What's proven in PASS;*
is proven on the streets.

to degrade & destroy Americans.

You see, given the easiness of their absolute jobs over courts, feeding them makes them too aggressive. Especially when their prey are helplessly dependent on them. And especially when their prey are intellectually bleeding uncontrollably at the same time.

For that's when the sharks are known to go into frenzy.

You see, theirs is staged to be a dividing practice. It's compulsive by nature to ensure dividing. That's their livelihood.

Theirs is a dividing motor that's upheld. An instinctive dividing motor that's literally enforced.

For they fight each other figuratively. While human beings are just inherently figuratively and/or literally collaterally damaged.

All knowledge, truth and understanding are thrown out the window when barbaric, animalistic instincts ravage the throttle and intentionally divides people simply by swerving the steering wheel any which way but straight.

Any and all civilized people become uncivilized animals flopping on the deck of an out-of-control speed boat when

forced on board of this crazy fishing
excursion.

Yes, when they cause wounds in their
helplessly dependent victims they can &
will go into frenzy. A frenzy that only
bolsters themselves at only their
victimized victim's expense. There's just
no other way on board of their system.

And what's worse is this is enforced. Enforced also at the expense of
their helplessly dependent victimized
victims.

May God help us all.

"The sense of doing good, the
satisfaction of being right, the joy of
looking favorably upon oneself, dear sir,
are powerful levers for keeping us upright and making us progress. On the
other hand, if men are deprived of that
feeling, they are changed into rabid
dogs."
     - Albert Camus

The United States Constitution
clearly & undeniably ORDERS that **"all"**
cases (people going through trials in
their life) equal a Democratic **"jury"**
rule.

Most people would agree that accepting the wise counsel of many is far su-

perior than accepting the condemner's counsel of one distraction fighting against another through games that they inherently have to play just to compete since it is a scientifically impossible system that they're using.

"Where no counsel is, the people fall; but in the multitude of counselors there is safety."
 - Proverbs 11:14

No truer words should ever be en-forced.

Manipulating the fact that **"all"** cases equal a Democratic **"jury"** decision is the difference between a legitimate Democracy ruling alongside the People and an illegitimate Dictatorship ruling over the People.
Yep, the bullies got us.
Especially since the option to amend that Right is right there for exercise. But it is routinely neglected instead.

"Infirmity doth still neglect all office where to our health is bound; we

What's gamed in court;
is forced onto the streets.
28
What's proven in PASS;
is proven on the streets.

are not ourselves when nature, being
oppressed, commands the mind to suffer
the body."
- *Shakespeare*

Neglect is the difference today
between an exclusive enterprise freely
exploiting the People, and inclusive
People freely serving People.
Covering up that manipulation and
all of the misleadings that *"must"* accom-
pany it is the difference between exclusive enforcements and inclusive enforcements. It is the difference between inclusively serving the People and exclusively exploiting the People more than
double exponentially times negatively.
The intellectually excluded are as
intellectually excluders do to them under
these terms. And with force if need be.
There is just no other way around it in
systems like this.
And this exclusive dumbing-down of
America has no chance or choice when it's
upon us under duress (threat.)
And protecting those cover-ups is
the difference between the good attributes of freedom and the now unquenchable
need for more and more traps in violation
that inherently curses all of humanity
subject to inhumanities at the same time

just to protect them. Inherently subject-
ing sanity to insanity.

The excluded are forced to be
subject to the dumbest today.

Inherently rendering all of us under
the duress of, and/or enforced to be the
dumbest in the world.

And knowing the difference between
exclusively exploiting the People &
inclusively serving the People has proven
to be more than double exponentially
times worse than a crime today.

Odds are that if you were to civilize sharks then they probably wouldn't
sever off the hands that feed them. Let
alone trap them into violations.

And fish sure wouldn't entrap to
enslave and/or consume each other like
shark practices do.

Judicial sharks presume that they
can take as much as they want to and get
away with it as long as they want to.
After all, that's what they do.

Well, I've got a "*trap*" for them.
And it's called the Truth.

The Truth is their kryptonite. And
it can only be derived from faith, wisdom, knowledge and understanding. Five
positive attributes that are not allowed
in court for lack thereof.

So I'll teach you why you should
never, ever feed the sharks in Illinois.

What's gamed in court;
is forced onto the streets.   30   *What's proven in PASS;*
is proven on the streets.

2. Growing fuel for motor boats

"Happiness depends upon ourselves."
- *Aristotle*

Since planting & growing Dictative powers is legal in America while planting & growing Democracy Powers is illegal, and I'm lower than fish food anyway, why should I stand by in idle allegiance to not only corruption, but to the enforced wasting, corrupting and violating of others by and for Dictator Rules?

Dictator Rules obviously enslave humanity and sanity subject to someone else's inhumanity and insanity. It doesn't make any sane sense.

And I would be un-American, inhumane & insane too just go along with that sort of wasting, corrupting and violating without opposing it.

I understand that having never

What's gamed in court;
is forced onto the streets. 31 *What's proven in PASS;*
is proven on the streets.

legitimately experienced this that many people cannot legitimately understand it.

Legally, my stance has to seem illegal. But I assure you and will show you that what the bullies do is real.

In fact, anyone can also find out for themselves.

But I for one pledged allegiance to the United States of American. And to the Republic (where representatives of We the People are elected to exercise power) for which it stands.

Not to exclusive sharks planting and growing the same for food for boat fuel while weeding out the good and healthy.

Today, judicial and national sharks have me snared with *"inferior"* bait and/or subjugating clothing to match if I simply don't agree with them.

But I am not the criminal here.

"Power does not corrupt men; fools, however, if they get into power, corrupt power."
 - *George Bernard Shaw*

Today, I am routinely, even compuls- ively framed as the *"criminal"* simply because I won't compromise, I won't conspire and I won't neglect wasting, corrupting and violating our most vulnerable children, our most valuable resources, and our most viable institutions.

"Power tends to corrupt and absolute power absolutely corrupts."
- *Lord Action*

Today, their business is to make everyone & everything subject to their brand of corrupting, their way of assuming, or else be forced to bow-down and serve corrupting. That's their feeding grounds. And that's their grounds for feeding.

"Fear corrupts... perhaps the fear of loss of power."
- *John Steinbeck*

Dictatorships with enforced hidden suppressing and/or traumatizing abilities (static ordered external dynamics) at their fingertips are much worse than one single Dictator alone. Because multiple Dictators can & will force you to comply with even impossible to comply with Rule, rules & rulers even without taking

What's gamed in court;
is forced onto the streets.   33   *What's proven in PASS;*
                                        is proven on the streets.

reality into consideration.

Yes, you may be subject to impossible to follow rules enforced from detached from reality positions unspeakably. And all by & for ulterior motives.

Pre-World War II Germans were fortunate compared to the American automation motor mechanically victimizing victims with its inherent 21st Century Crucifixions. It is a beast!

"Never be bullied into silence. Never allow yourself to be made a victim. Accept no one's definition of your life; define yourself."
- *Harvey Fierstein*

Illegitimate judicial superiors practice, uphold and enforce that We the People can't legally act as legitimate fathers.

The obvious STD (Static-Transforming Dynamics) agenda is to make everyone subject to them (knowing full well that only they are detached from reality) or else we'll be "*tricked*" and/or Forced into being subject to their STD.

Why? Because there is easy money <u>and</u> absolute power not only in it, but even more in neglecting it. That's a true bully's paradise.

Illegitimate judicial superiors practice, uphold & enforce that we can't legally act as legitimate Constitutional Americans.

The obvious agenda (STD) is that everyone either accept it, be figuratively tricked into accepting it, and/or else be literally forced into serving their brand of treason.

Why? Because there is easy money <u>and</u> absolute power not only in it, but even more in neglecting it.

And magical "*interpretations*" are irrelevant when actions speak louder than words.

Illegitimate judicial superiors practice, uphold & enforce that we can't legally act as legitimate Christians. As children of the light. As children of the truth. As children of the Way to Heaven.

The obvious agenda (STD) is to make everyone subject to sin, or else they're forced to serve sin.

Why? Because there is easy money <u>and</u> absolute power not only in it, but even more in neglecting it.

Above all its fraud.

Some say that you reap what you sow.

While others say that you get run over by what you stole.

    "Governments that block the aspirations of their people, that steal or are corrupt, that oppress and torture or that deny freedom of expression and human rights should bear in mind that they will find it increasingly hard to escape the judgment of their own people...."
    - *William Hague*

3. Plastic bait or real live human beings?

"Joy is a net of love by which you can catch souls."
- *Mother Teresa*

Plastic bait "*versus*" real live human beings:
On one hand, they sent me to prison for trying to uphold the law and protect real people instead of the attorney's impossibly crooked practice ruling over a silly little piece of plastic.
On the other hand, I found out the real way that their silly little plastic bait is meant to catch victims into their own, automatically victimizing Death Trap.

Oh... the pain and suffering of their excluding quagmires!

What's gamed in court;
is forced onto the streets.   37   *What's proven in PASS;*
is proven on the streets.

You see, they sent me to prison for following the law. That's how far hell-bent that they have become.

The Truth isn't the only thing that is worse than a crime anymore.

Following the law is actually worse than a crime too if they are the ones violating it.

The fact is that they do not uphold "*justice for all*" as they claim.

And they really do not uphold humanity.

It's now proven scientifically that they only uphold their trade regardless. Often in permanent and perpetual pain and suffering for their victimized victims who then have no acceptable outlet to even question back.

They uphold "*stuff*" for themselves. And they uphold nothing for the humanity or the sanity of the rest of us.

On one hand we have non-human Rights. On the other hand we have non-human Rights absolutely murdering human needs.

The sharks protect plastic and/or delusional bait used to lure human beings by their own inspired executive and/or legislative powers to fall into their vortex hole. A legitimate Death Trap.

So I protect human beings by trapping sharks to paper.

I figure that this is how one tries to catch and release life away from Death's grip.

Another example of my shark fishing expedition is that judges obviously have tools of their trade and a personal life too.

I try to trap the tools and not the personal human being.

Which is the opposite of them.

They trap humans and not tools.

They choose to punish human beings and not things.

In fact, they'll uphold things at the expense, pain and suffering of human beings.

Their victims have no choice. We are forced to be likewise victimized twisted.

Yet the abusers have a choice.

They don't have to victimize their own victims. Yet they do.

My mentors of the United States Constitution helped me to see the light. So I choose to punish things and not people. (Even though that backfires on me in their courts.)

I try to uphold higher standards. Especially those with known healing

solutions. While both higher standards
and healing solutions naturally incubates
truth, love and life.

Bad for their business, profit
margins and/or political advantages. But
good for life, efficiency and reality.

This is how one floats to the top
after being almost dead, lower than fish
food and torn to shreds after being force
fed to sharks.

It's time to warn others.

And this should allow legitimate
Democracy Powers (people & the People) to
grow, to unite, to strengthen and to
heal.

And this should also allow illegitimate Dictative Powers to slow, dissolve
and hurt. (Especially those which most
victimize their own victims.)

After all, what's worse than hating
people? Forcing people to bow-down a
little, or else to bow-down a lot with
automatic Rule, rules & rulers that bait
us into a Death Trap that renders us
crazy and inhumane at the same time with
its insane inhumanity.

This is the direct result of dictating fiction over nonfiction.

Dictating fiction over nonfiction is
eventually Catastrophic.

Dictating fiction over nonfiction is
figuratively and/or literally forcing

What's gamed in court;
is forced onto the streets.   40   *What's proven in PASS;*
is proven on the streets.

people insane and inhumane. There is no other option.

And it's well-known that those doing it do know this.

For this is how they themselves choose to subjugate people.

And it is becoming well-known that they neglect this as well. That they neglect the consequences to their own actions and simply keep doing it "*worse*" under duress and/or Worse with force.

But realizing this should now help us avoid further Catastrophes. And will help heal the wounds caused by those Catastrophes.

Realizing this, however, is very, very difficult today.

Realizing this is absolutely a blessing from God Himself.

But there should be no more ignoring it either way.

Why ignore quagmires (difficult situations to get out of?) When there's so much opportunity to advance learning in solving them? And when they are so much fun to beat?!

What's gamed in court;
is forced onto the streets.   41   *What's proven in PASS;*
is proven on the streets.

Sharks hide in their own insulated places to exploit ultimate dilemmas that governing quagmires create. (Plastic bait and/or paper lines for human food, that is.)

And the sharks expect us to pay for it all and to suffer from it all irreparably and without accountability. (Stupid bullies!)

So we're literally lower than fish food by the seeds of another in order to feed the sharks who simply have to have someone else wiggle the bait so that they can run over us with their boat motor.

The objective from the seeds of fuel for their motor boats is that heads or tails tricksters win. While heads or tails everyone else is either the duress or under the duress to lose.

It's not "*justice for all.*" It's, "they always win, and the rest of us always loose" no matter what.

Paper or plastic bait for inhuman sharks growing humans to be used for fuel for their MMD (Motor of Mass Destruction) boat is the swamp today that some people call the USA.

The Law Doctor

"And this is the condemnation, that the light has come into the world, and men loved the absence of light rather than light, because their deeds were evil.

"For everyone practicing evil hates the light and does not come to light, lest their deeds should be exposed.

"But he who does the truth comes to the light, that his deeds may be clearly seen, that they have been done in God (who is Love.)

– *Jesus Christ*

What's gamed in court;
is forced onto the streets.   43   *What's proven in PASS;*
is proven on the streets.

The Law Doctor

4. Scientific Conviction that a needlessly wasting, corrupting & violating conspiracy has undermined to overthrow governments

{Permanent & perpetual, indisputably established proof that a current group of fraudulent authorizers have conspired together to first undermine and then to overthrow governments and the People as we should know it.}

"Where justice is denied, where poverty is enforced, where ignorance prevails, and where any one class is made to feel that society is an organized conspiracy to oppress, rob and degrade them, neither persons nor property will be safe."
- Frederick Douglass

When the fact is that it's inherently punished worse than a crime to in-

What's gamed in court;
is forced onto the streets.   45   *What's proven in PASS;*
is proven on the streets.

stinctively protect one's self from obvious motorized abuse then something is wrong with the systems, not the people.

For example, if what you are doing is wrong then that's on you.

Unless I know that it's wrong too. Because then it's on both of us only if I ignore it.

But if I try to correct it then it's only on the violator.

If the obvious violator puts me in prison for being responsible and trying to fix it then that's on both of us if I let him.

But if I fight back then it's solely on them regardless of the outcome.

Government decisions (including juries & Democracies) are always subverted today away from reality and into exclusive, reality-detached, delusioning courts in order to overthrow their own victims.

Everything and everyone is overthrown inside of an exclusive Tripolar Weegie Wedging in Court. An intimidating Compulsively Dividing-Vices Device (CD-VD.) CD-VD presses out money and power from us to them.

Infecting us all with STD's.

"The church disowned, the tower

overthrown, the bells upturned, what have
we to do(;)
    "But stand with empty hands and
palms turned upwards(;)
    "In an age which advances progres-
sively backwards?"
    – *T. S. Eliot*

    Government is undermined and over-
thrown by an exclusively licensed association of judges & attorneys.
    Bar associates, and those serving
them instead of our People, have let our
country down. They've let our People go.
    Bar associated judges and attorneys
are in fact a known brainwashing group.
They are even known to be brainwashed
themselves. They have no choice. They are
really detached from reality. So that's
all on them.
    And they are known to practice and
uphold Leverage as somehow magically
being "*law*" regardless of the irreparable
consequences that this Ultimate Quagmire
(UQ) inherently causes. Regardless of the
irreparable corrupting that this UQ inherently forces on helplessly dependent
systems. And regardless of the irreparable inhumanity and insanity that this
forces on the victimized people and the
victimized professionals alike.

What's gamed in court;
is forced onto the streets.   47   *What's proven in PASS;*
                                                   is proven on the streets.

Please pray for us all. Insanity times inhumanity is at the wheel!

The STD has a proven hidden agenda. Which is not only to profiteer off of the same betraying, but to persuade and/or push as much hidden "*law*" (Leverage) as it possibly can get away with. That's all it's programmed to do!

"Secrecy, being an instrument of conspiracy, ought never to be the system of a regular government."
- *Jeremy Bentham*

An unfortunate practice that together upholds absolutely foreign (to the People), alienating (within the People) Leverages fronting as "*law.*"

"Alienation as our present destiny is achieved only by outrageous violence perpetuated by human beings on human beings."
- *R.D. Laing*

They are known to pressure one group of People with absolute Leverage, and the other group of People towards absolute "*law*" defects in order to keep them in-

What's gamed in court;
is forced onto the streets. 48 *What's proven in PASS;*
is proven on the streets.

tentionally separated and at most potentially violating odds.

The STD's CD-VD (Compulsively Dividing-Vices Device) divides the People financially, psychologically and/or physically while it renders those protecting it the untouchable independent authorizers.

Thus, they are the secret controlling factor with their own immunity.

Together they uphold foreign and alienating mechanics, or static dynamics, fronting as "*law*" instead of their own sworn allegiance to submit themselves to the United States Constitution Bill of Rights Due Process for all. And regardless of the State, Federal, Human & Sane Rights that this violates.

For example, on May 14, 2013 during court in Montgomery County, Illinois on case number 12-CF-178 I asked the judge, "are you going to sentence me?"

The judge said, "Yes."

I said, "(because) if the same official that I've accused of a crime (and it was in the case file that I had accused him of many crimes) is going to sentence me then that's indisputable proof of a Hierarchy (as directly opposed to even a Democracy.)

I said that, "my Rights under the authority of the United States Consti-

What's gamed in court;
is forced onto the streets.   49   *What's proven in PASS;*
is proven on the streets.

tution grants me protection from that sort of 'process.' My Rights under the authority of the Illinois Constitution secures me to reasonable protection from the accused. The only reasonable protection would be for this courts associates to publicly accept my Deceleration of Independence. This would leave me free to pursue my mission to live a Constitutional life and pursue new engineered Laws void of Catch-22's. And it would leave Illinois State Bar Associates (ISBA) free to do what they do (serve Catch-22's.) This reasonable protection also aligns with all (ISBA) court associates who swore to uphold the United States Constitution supreme."

If the same person that I've accused of a crime is going to sentence me then that's their own precedence that rapists now have permission to sentence their own victims. And that those who are criminally accused now have the grounds to victimize their own victims.

"There's only one way left to escape the alienation of present day society: to retreat ahead of it."
 - *Roland Barthes*

The ISBA judge gave me three years in prison for trying to follow State

Statutes, the Illinois Constitution, the
United States Constitution, their own
oaths, and even their common practice
that's upheld.

Three years in prison for not
conspiring with their "*state*" bait and
Leverage switch.

All by and for an exclusive Hierarchy that dwarfs our Rights & their
Responsibilities.

"You cannot escape the responsibility of tomorrow by evading it today."
- *Abraham Lincoln*

ISBA members are an exclusively
licensed stronghold (a place that serves
as either the center of a group or of
persons holding a controversial
viewpoint) over people & the People.

Some would say that it feels like
weegie-magic onto the rest of us.

But I think that we can all agree
that it is an exclusively licensed
umbrella of final power and final profit
over everything & everyone else.

No other type of practice is even
legitimately accepted within "there"
stronghold to help people & the People in
the final authority of government except

What's gamed in court;
is forced onto the streets.   51   *What's proven in PASS;*
is proven on the streets.

Bar associates since they rule & roost in our judiciary and beyond.

The strongholds of another can never be of my father.

And they'll never tell people this, but it's now been scientifically convicted that theirs is not only brokering leverage & hedging disorder, but it's hiding brokering leverage and causing disorder. It's not "*law and order.*" That's the machination (mak'i na shun.)

And not just simply hiding leverage and hedging disorder. But hiding leverage and causing disorder hidden behind "*law and order.*" The ultimate betrayal! The ultimate human eating machine!

"Hypocrisy can afford to be magnificent in its promises, for never intending to go beyond promise, it costs nothing."

- *Edmond Burke*

And not just simply hiding leverage and causing disorder behind "*law and order,*" but neglecting to warn us that it's leverage and disorder that they're hiding behind "*law and order!*"

How can we protect ourselves? We

What's gamed in court;
is forced onto the streets.   52   *What's proven in PASS;*
is proven on the streets.

can't. We can't even know.

So what? Are we not good enough to even be able to know this quagmire exists so that we can at least make an informed decision if we ever have to protect ourselves or our children in court? Or if somebody files a suit against us in court? Are we just supposed to be slaves to ignorance? (Because that's what their gross neglect does.) With literal bars and guns and tasers and chains and pepper spray to back it up if need be?!

One has to ask themselves when they are being exploited, why are they being exploited. And if the answer is because of their own lack of knowledge, then that is on them. But if the answer is because of the lack of knowledge tricked and/or forced onto them, well, then that's on the beast.

When you exploit people and the People for lack of knowledge and you literally force them to lack knowledge then what outcome can you expect?!

So, since that is the way that it is, and all judges & attorneys took an oath under God obligating themselves to be subject to the United States Constitution, and implied that they are all subject to God, then I'm going to have to comply with their most serious of intentions and hold them accountable for having overthrown governments and knowledge alike.

I'm holding them accountable for having undermined and overthrown governments and knowledge both by intentionally misleading the People.

"Who went into the witches den and came out alive? The witch!"

Obviously, they don't have the sanity or the mental capacity to make any decisions truthfully. Especially when it comes to making decisions for other people. And especially since they are fully vested and well versed in trickery just to "*protect*" their jobs.

"We must no longer be children, tossed to and fro and blown about by every wind of doctrine, by people's trickery, by their craftiness in deceitful scheming."
- *Ephesians 4:14*

Like good versus bad there are fundamental, foundational, structural, inherent & financial differences between scientific engineers and chaotic

What's gamed in court;
is forced onto the streets.　　　54　　　*What's proven in PASS;*
is proven on the streets.

attorneys.

"The engineer, and more generally the designer, is concerned with how things ought to be - how they ought to be in order to attain goals, and to function."
- *Herbert Simon*

Engineers are indoctrinated, vested and profit according to how well they unite pieces together to professionally build things upright.

Attorneys on the other hand, are indoctrinated, vested and profit according to how "*well*" they divide pieces apart to professionally tear things down-low.

Are we the United States of America or the Dividing State Bars of America?

"I think patriotism is like charity- it begins at home."
- *Henry Adams*

Engineers are known to design pieces in order to unite lasting, monumental and meaningful projects.

Attorneys on the other hand, are known to design pieces in order to divide lasting, monumental and meaningful destruction's.

Engineers and attorneys are known not to see eye-to-eye. In fact, our minds are flipped upside down and inverse of one another.

The difference between engineers and attorneys can be summed up in that one is upright, while the other is well bent.

Governments today, unfortunately, reflect the later.

Attorneys leverage fear & conflicts of interests into officers & officials to neglect and/or punish people for living according to the exact same standards and principles that they themselves swore to uphold.

While engineers have no capacity but to erase this type of error and start all over.

Otherwise, it's the designers who are held liable if the system falls and hurts people. And theirs is obviously designed for Catastrophe.

For attorneys, innocent people must be punished and their families suffer to cover-up practice mistakes simply to keep the vice of solidarity intact for power, profit and/or vanity.

While the sheer magnitude of this

type of universal handicap and worthless suppression just blows the minds of engineers due to the ease, but refusal of the practice to understand the permanent & perpetual consequences that this has on helpless but dependent victimized victims and their innocent young children alike.

For attorneys, this type of sneaky snake setting up and/or scorpion-like backstabbing is profiteering. It's *"working their way to the top," "job security"* and growing their own market share.

For engineers, "what the Hell!?"

Theirs is like classic bait-and-switch tactics. Or, Rope-a-Dope operations. Illegal to any other trade. But common tactics also used by thugs, bullies, hustlers, murderers, swindlers and pimps.

Only theirs is even worse. Theirs is to bait-and-then-permanently-perpetually-punish-and-switch unspeakably.

People and the People today have no choice but to accept whatever judges and attorneys tell us. We're helplessly dependent under their own brand of exclusive authorizing power.

To them, all people are not equal. They trick and/or physically treat us in order to make themselves superior. And so that we all must be dependent on them. And so that we all must pay them their price. And so that everyone but them must pay and suffer from their mistakes.

Engineers on the other hand have to be upfront, fair and level. If not our projects come out exactly like they were planned. There's no denying accountability. It is accountability.

"When a train goes through a tunnel and it gets dark, you don't throw away your ticket and jump off. You sit still and trust the engineer."
- *Corrie Ten Boom*

"When you see an electrically generated roller coaster take off at super-speeds in nanoseconds to heights never seen before and then it flies through loops and a tunnel and things get dizzy and dark, you can either throw away your ticket or not, turn the switch off or not, but in every and all ways you are getting off that train safely. Even whether you see or trust the engineer or not."
- *Aaron W. Wemple*

Facts are facts. But being lost in the lack of facts is being lost in the lack of facts.

What's gamed in court;
is forced onto the streets.   58   *What's proven in PASS;*
is proven on the streets.

Nonfiction is nonfiction.

What was supposed to be a government
with officials who had no choice but to
be responsible, and a People with undeniable United States Constitutional Bill of
Rights Due Process paid in full is now
instead the undeniable smoke & mirrors
show from an excluding extortion racket
exploiting the People into the ground
hovering themselves over us supreme.
    A most foreign and alienating bus-
iness practice. A practice of stretching
"*law*" (hiding leverage) just as far and
as wide as the other eyes can't see.
    While the will and good of the
People are null and void mute issues.
Inherently run into the ground and/or
"*raised to the roof*" (RUN INTO THE GROUND
WITH FORCE!)

    "Whether you're on a train or not,
in some systems that you're railroaded
through you're getting run over or 'not.'
But you are getting run over."
    - *Victims of the Bar's train ride.*

In my case number 12-CF-178 for
example, less than 1% of their "*process*"
(officer pressure and professional

What's gamed in court;
is forced onto the streets. 59 *What's proven in PASS;*
is proven on the streets.

persuasion) included an unbiased Democratic jury trial. While over 99% of my
"*process*" (officer pressure and
professional psychiatric persuasion) was
Dictated behind closed doors with extortive and exploitative leverage intentionally in mind.

Of course people in jail are very
easy to trick and to take advantage of.
We're helplessly dependent on it!

People on the streets are almost
just as easy to game given that court and
their staged prestige are so intimidating
and/or flattering.

"The disfranchisement of a legal
elector by fraud or intimidation is a
crime too grave to be regarded lightly."
 - *Benjamin Harrison*

Their "*process*" (literal Leverage &
figurative "*leverage*") was itself Cruel &
Unusual punishment.

The jury was rendered irrelevant.

I was set-up to fail or else fail
worse the harder that I tried.

And all before the trial even began.

This is their MO. And it's called
setting up the Death Trap under duress of
the same with staged positions. It's

What's gamed in court;
is forced onto the streets.   60   *What's proven in PASS;*
is proven on the streets.

academic.

I had already suffered from 124 days in jail, and 124 days of my life ruined and my children wounded for life by the time that their trial rolled around.

A trial simply for not buying into their brand of bait while trying to Duly Processing my accusations against them civilly.

"You must be the change you wish to see in the world."
- *Mahatma Gandhi*

It is figuratively and literally impossible for the rest of us to understand their delusional, detached from reality need to ruin other people's real lives forever over their illegitimately gotten gains.

Where's the humanity?
Where's the humility?
Where's the sanity?
Who's the boss here? Humans or non-humans? Sanity or insanity? The tricky Hierarchy or the honest people?

"Insanity: doing the same thing over and over again and expecting different results." - *Albert Einstein*

What's gamed in court;
is forced onto the streets.   61   *What's proven in PASS;*
is proven on the streets.

It's impossible to support an excluding group who demands support or else their victims are set up to fail. Their victims are premeditated set up to be victimized if they don't cave in.

"Promises are like crying babies in a movie theater, they should be carried out at once."
   - *Norman Vincent Peale*

The jury in my Case and now Cause was rendered irrelevant anyway since actors who were also detached from reality had been coached with legal authority (which implies that it's illegal to defy) behind the scenes, since rumors were planted with legal authority (which implies that they are illegal to defy), words were put into my "*mouth*" on illegitimate professional reports, and accused "*cover-ups*" were professionally "*protected*" with the same pattern of Civil Rights abuse & inhumane treatment that I was complaining about in civil court first before this new pattern of Civil Rights abuse and inhumane treatment began murdering me.

The same pattern of civil Rights abuse and inhumane treatment that forced me to declare my independence from this unaccountable permanent and perpetual drain of abuse over the world.

All the while first-hand officer's eye-witness proof that courts cause Intolerable Repressive Effects (IRE) were simply punished until they went away.

Which is like whipping a crying baby to get the victim to stop crying.

"Whipping and abuse are like laudanum: you have to double the dose as the sensibilities decline."
- *Harriet Beecher Stowe*

It's no wonder that so many people die under this neglectful and/or worse authorization "*process*."

The guards of this 21st Century Concentration Camp even know the drill.

"You've got to stop whipping a dead horse sometime."
- *Jim Knight*

My "*process*" (Psychotic Pressure & Sociopathic Persuasion) was that I was forced to be demoralized, dehumanized & deteriorated professionally, physically, financially, relationally & mentally by the time that trial had rolled around

(124 days later.) And all the while I was supposedly "*innocent.*"

I would have easily been taken advantage of had I even been able to participate in the trial. But why conspire with corrupting other professions and abusing victimized victims even if I was able?

"Do not envy the violent and do not choose any of their ways."
- *Proverbs 3:31*

I for one upheld the law and life by refusing to be an accomplice to self-evident violations of law and life.

And I was forced to Scientifically Convicted them with having Overthrown Governments.

All the while I lost everything and almost everyone trying to follow to law.

"A man who was completely innocent, offered himself as a sacrifice for the good of others, including his enemies, and became ransom of the world. It was a perfect act."
- *Mahatma Gandhi*

What's gamed in court;
is forced onto the streets.   64   *What's proven in PASS;*
is proven on the streets.

"Follow me, and I will make you fishers of men."
- *Jesus Christ*

"I am the WAY, the TRUTH, and the LIFE.
No one comes to the FATHER but by me."
- *Jesus Christ*

Anyway, could an association like accountants legally band together in a pyramid weegie-like stronghold to exclusively license themselves in order that only they could decide dividing Leverage people and "*law*" victims into prison for not paying the going rate just to follow any "*process*" that themselves authorize?
Of course not.
Could plumbers, carpenters or electricians? Of course not.
Or, could other trades victimize people who claimed to be their victims?
It's like insider trading on Wall Street, only it's Much "*much*" worse. It's more than double exponentially times worse than insider trading on Wall Street.
It's illegal for everyone and everything else. But if you show them that what they are doing is illegal then they will punish you and make you and

What's gamed in court;
is forced onto the streets.   65   *What's proven in PASS;*
is proven on the streets.

yours suffer forever for it.

As proof, punishments today never fit the crime. It fits their profit margins and/or political ambitions.

A recent Goldman Sachs investor was found liable for misleading investors.

Per court order, he would have gotten a promotion had he punished the victims for claiming to be victims.

"True patriotism hates injustice in its own land more than anywhere else."
- *Clarence Darrow*

Unfortunately, theirs is a Cruel & Unusual "*process*," regardless of guilt or innocence, man or woman, child or issue.

In reality it doesn't have to be. It's not supposed to be.

But for business it's ideal leverage to "*hide*" and/or Leverage.

But it's not leading by sworn Responsibility to citizen Rights that we're all led to believe to be paying our taxes for.

"This nation will remain the land of the free only so long as it is home of the brave." - *Elmer Davis*

What's gamed in court;
is forced onto the streets.   66   *What's proven in PASS;*
is proven on the streets.

In a pattern of similar vice and/or vising "*processes*," local officers & officials are rendered null and void with ISBA judges & attorney's authorizing the rules of the roads ahead of us.

Or at best, officers & officials are just used for leverage if & when a judge or attorney needs them.

It's the same pattern of protecting bullies at their own victim's expense. Or of puppet masters and their helplessly dependent puppets. Or of hushing an accuser.

It's the same thing. It's just different circumstances.

Likewise, State Representatives can be rendered null & void, dependent on supporting judges and attorneys who authorize Bills before and after votes.

And during conflicts debating votes.

If there is a prized debate, whether real or tricked, it actually drums up business <u>and</u> perceived authority for those authorizing in the excluding judi-cial branch.

Both of which, profit <u>and</u> power, are irreversible. Also due to the Leverage "*process*." No matter if gains were from a trick or not.

Since theirs is a business of disorder all they have to do is find someone's prize pride and stir with it for a while in order to build profit <u>and</u> power.

And the bigger the prize the easier it is to stir people up over it by simply ordering disorder legislation.

Sometimes all that it takes just is a little tickle.

Sometimes it takes a staged fight.

But it always begins ahead of time with trickery. And that's their only mainstay.

The quagmire that our governments are now in is exactly why our Forefathers left corrupting and abusing authority.

Avoiding UQ (the Ultimate Quagmire) is exactly why they ORDERED three branches of government.

And it's exactly why the three branches of government were meant to check and balance each other equally. To keep them all level.

Not one branch with one exclusive group hiding directions supreme.

And definitely not one exclusive enterprise stretching themselves out gaining power <u>and</u> profit from within all three branches of government with a hidden weapon that no one else is allowed to use in the highest and only branch of authority.

"Sure, bring all your problems to us. And if we can't solve 'em then we sure as Hell can '*solve*' them. And if you can't agree that we '*solved*' them then we sure as Hell can divide and conquer you too until you do!"
    - *Anonymous licensed attorney/judge*

According to the Illinois Government Handbook State Representatives have authority over judges.

But due to a recent vote, and a conflict of interest that locks it in, judges now have implicated authority over State Representatives.

By and for the known vice vising device from "*hiding*" Leverage, judges have brokered greater authority because of a conflict of interest ruse stirred up during a recent (summer 2013) pension reduction debate.

Judges were blessed with power <u>and</u> profit by being excluded from the proposed pension reduction issue due to a "*conflict of interest*" scheme if a civil suit happened to prevail. (Yet Constitutionally, a jury is legitimate authority. Not a Dictator.)

And these tricks are getting worse and worse.

Undermining people for leverage knowing that they'll be overridden in court is what attorney's practice.

Overriding everything and everyone on behalf of their fellow attorney's brokering power <u>and</u> hedging profit while being the most delusionally detached from reality is the judges Rule.

But this is really very seriously dangerous.

"He's really sort of the devil. He's completely emotionally detached. He has no empathy. You find that on psychopaths."
- *Ralph Fiennes*

Like our local jury and state governments, our Democracies of elections are rendered null, void and/or "*worse*" since judges and attorneys have the only authorizing seats that ultimately matter.

And since they have the only enforced authority over the People's Democracy before, during and after any election.

Not to mention that they are the only ones who even have a remote possibility to interpret the meaning of governing words in Bills, Statutes, Policies, Practice's and enforcements.

Of course interpretations and "*interpretations*" always fit the business

What's gamed in court;
is forced onto the streets.   70   *What's proven in PASS;*
is proven on the streets.

of stretching hidden leverage for increased disorder. They would have to literally be insane not to.

Why wouldn't they put questionable words into law? Why wouldn't they put up legal fences just to take them down, paint them a different color, and put them back up again? Why wouldn't they put up policies and practices and enforcements just to take them down or re-arrange them? Paint them a different color, victimize different victims, detour people where ever for "*whatever*" and promote their own business and protect themselves and destroy any opponents and promote themselves all at the same time and all at the same expense and suffering of the exploited people?!

Especially since there's no one else who can authorize force domestically against them.

If people can't just magically understand the permanent and perpetual Rope-a-Dope practice [and "*legally*" (Leveraging-ly) we're not allowed to] then they can and will be punished in a court of "*law.*"

Thus, their rates can and will be whatever just as long as they all stick together.

Because only they matter ultimately in court.

What's gamed in court;
is forced onto the streets.
    71
What's proven in PASS;
is proven on the streets.

So when the charges swell (and why wouldn't they) they do well.

And when the "*hidden*" (Leverage) divisions grow we the blind People get rolled.

We're helpless <u>and</u> dependent. Helplessly dependent on swelling delusional charges and growing "*law*" (Leverage) DIVISIONS. Divisions that inherently steal, kill and destroy.

Likewise, helplessness is being created, prorated, mentally handicapped, physically repressed, intellectually suppressed, physically and intellectually traumatized, lives ruined, and children's lives even greater helplessly ruined dependently simply for not being able to conspire with judges and attorneys.

If We the People can't just magically submit to their weapon of choice on their own terms in their pulpit with their own magic spells that only they can cast then they can and will unite to be the ruling force deciding amongst themselves to take advantage of us all in way too many ways.

People are helpless <u>and</u> dependent in their power <u>and</u> profit arena.

We're just slaves to fit their detached presumptions. Vexed and/or vised if necessary.

People are helpless and hopeless

under their Rule. We're in no position to barter.

People are enslaved to even our own devices not having an acceptable free-will voice to fight back. Because their weapon is supreme and we must swallow "*whatever*" it spits out.

They are known to professionally brainwash their own victims to death. Men, women and children alike.

"Power always thinks... that it is doing God's service when it is violating all his laws."
- *John Adams*

What's gamed in court;
is forced onto the streets.   73   *What's proven in PASS;*
is proven on the streets.

The Law Doctor

Bait or Beings?

Is Illinois a crafty Hierarchy authorizing authority? Or a legitimate Democracy authorizing authority?

What enterprise has all of the recent Bills, policies, practices and fighting helped? On the front and the back side of the People?

Who have all of the recent bills, policies, practices and fighting hurt? On the front and the back side of any vote?

What enterprise did all of the "*process*" promoting the same learn from in order to be the "*law*" (Leverage) down in reality in America?

The Disordering Leverage Association (DLA) has a well-known history of undermining everything and everyone in order to assume their own authority when it matters with force. Even over our officers and our officials.

Judges and attorneys have a well-known history of working together to undermine and then to override everything and everyone else. Which intentionally handicaps the best and brightest minds and professions.

The DLA intentionally handicaps the best and brightest nation towards the pit.

All before, during and after any

What's gamed in court;
is forced onto the streets. 75 *What's proven in PASS;*
is proven on the streets.

Democratic decision. Which is truly a
mutiny.

Look, the fact is that there is only
one side of our issues with Bar
associate's detached from reality. And
it's not their victims.
But that detached-from-reality side
is the side that circuit clerks and
officers and officials bow down to.
That's the side of a bottomless pit.

Unfortunately for the real
helplessly dependent citizens, most
vulnerable young minds, and most valuable
institutions alike, disorder and error
just makes good DLA business sense.
And when an enterprise of leveraging
death and destruction for maximum profit
and power is riding on all of our backs,
then no one is safe.
When they have all authority and no
responsibilities, even over our police,
then they're not even safe from
themselves.

If a stronghold has you in a head-
lock then what choice do you really have?

What's gamed in court;
is forced onto the streets.   76   *What's proven in PASS;*
is proven on the streets.

Everyone knows that power drunk is much more dangerous than being money drunk or even love drunk. But if you're the subject of others being power drunk and money drunk plus them hating your love drunk and they're in control? Well, I hate being a passenger on that Jrunk Judicial train ride down into oblivion.

When one group has manipulated power and profit to control the one branch of now highest authority, at the expense of the other two branches, with their own exclusively licensed practice of hidden stretching leverage that is profitable with respect to just being foreign and alienating to everyone else, and they have fully vested, like-minded tentacles, who may not even know any better, activating in the legislative and executive branches of both State and Federal Government, then why wouldn't they repress people and hold us hostage for more money and more power?

That is their one and only business model.

And now with universal bindings (which can be real or made up), everyone and everything can be tickled or tricked into being helplessly dependent on the impossible Law of Leverage Disorder (LLD.)

LLD is known to cause ill psychological effects and ill physical defects.

Helpless Victimized Victims Disorder (HVVD) can be ordered through policy, leveraged through practice, upheld through rule, neglected through office and enforced through police without anyone being the wiser.

And if they are then the wiser are punished legitimately Worse and "*worse*" than a criminal. Or until they stay quiet about it. Or until they die.

Psychological warfare is the group's main trade. That's what they have to use in a court. And that's what's obviously detached from reality.

But their victims obviously feel the pressures both mentally and physically. It's illegal not to.

The Rights, Responsibilities, humanity and sanity of the rest of us are simply collateral damage to their detached games.

The collateral damages to men, women and children alike are all irrelevant to the delusioning standards of detached games that are being practiced and upheld.

But ask any engineer, theirs is <u>not</u> real Law. It's the opposite of Law. It's trickery. It's anti-law. Instead-of-law. Anything but Law.

It's a deceptive practice alienating people, coveting titles of foreign nobility, and pitting civil people's pride against each other increasing disorder.

Like instigating a dog fight and then collecting royalties from all bets. And from hedges to bets. And from hedges to hedges to bets. And from "*hedges*" to Hedges to bets. And furthermore forever. It doesn't stop. It just hurts worse and worse more than double exponentially forever.

Abusing power to create helplessness in order to take advantage of the instinctive helplessness that you've created is not only criminally corrupt, but corrupting to others who have no choice but to buy into it simply to compete.

It's leading people to fail while giving themselves immunity and money not only for misleading, but for processing the failure.

Which feels like getting stabbed in the back over and over and over again when you're on the receiving end.

It's like being imprisoned by the same people that you've accused of gang rapping you.

It's like everybody believing in their replaceable jobs more than in your

What's gamed in court;
is forced onto the streets.   79   *What's proven in PASS;*
is proven on the streets.

irreplaceable life.

It's like watching them laugh and buy cars and houses and enjoying their children while your life is ruined. And even your children have been alienated.

While everyone protects job titles no matter whom it is.

And nobody legitimately protects Human beings.

Likewise, the problem with funneling everything and everyone through the bottleneck of one brain in court is that anyone who hasn't been taught to think exactly the same way, or isn't in the same mood as the judge, can be punished for it.

For example, if my IQ is 120 and the judge's is 30, then only I can be the "*criminal.*"

If my IQ is 30 and the judge's is 120, only I'm the "*criminal.*"

If I'm happy and the judge is sad then I could be found guilty in a court of "*law.*"

Unfortunately, judges and attorneys are their own masters. (Though they oppose even themselves by oaths, documentations, statics, dynamics and affirmations.)

Judges unfortunately are an illegitimate seal of authority.

What's gamed in court;
is forced onto the streets.   80   *What's proven in PASS;*
is proven on the streets.

But the vial of attorney's are their associate's gatekeepers.

Officers, officials and the people either accept their misleading and impossible posture and/or persuasion, or else they can and will suffer the consequences of the automatic Motor of Mass Destruction (MMD.)

It's the "*greatest*" vessel to create, exploit and then extort benefits that the world has ever seen.

But this type of unconstitutional vising device with its posture and persuasion to pit people against each other is exactly why our forefathers lived and died to bless us with undeniable RIGHTS.

And it's exactly why our officials were to have undeniable RESPONSIBILITIES.

And this is exactly why People have the Right to protection from their accused.

This is exactly why titles of foreign nobility aren't to be recognized in America.

And this is exactly why the accused has undeniable RIGHT to face their accuser under the authority of a Democratic jury. (Unless it's Amended of course.)

Undeniable, unabridgeable and unconstruable RIGHTS that every citizen

What's gamed in court;
is forced onto the streets.   81   *What's proven in PASS;*
is proven on the streets.

is blessed with.

No one should have to go through a Conspiracy that has overthrown governments first.

But, if that's all it took to prove that I'm still dad, then I'd do it again in a heartbeat.

If that's all that it took to take back my moral RESPONSIBILITY then I'd do it again until my last dying breath.

And if that's all it took to defend the United States Constitution and my RIGHTS from absolutely ruthless bullies, then I'd do it again with every last bit of Free Speech that I can speak.

"Reality must take precedence over public relations, for nature cannot be fooled."
- Richard P. Feynman

I for one cannot just sit around in good conscious and neglect them misleading people and children under the impression that "this" (Tricky Force) is somehow law.

"This" (Force) just to trap naive, helpless and unassuming victims into being victimized. Simply because normal people have no way of knowing that it's

What's gamed in court;
is forced onto the streets.   82   *What's proven in PASS;*
is proven on the streets.

impossible to understand the Law and
Disorder of Leverage. Especially while
it's being hidden from us with such
intimidating force.

   And what's scary is that I did not
participate with their arrest, their
charges, their rituals, or their trial
because I had a known conflict pending,
but it still stuck. And that means that
they can now charge anybody with anything
and make it stick. Because they now have
their own precedence. And what they call
common '*law*' and case '*law*' alike has
held themselves that this is all that it
takes to forever exploit that routine.
   But what they call common "*law*" and
case "*law*" even has different meanings
depending on who uses it.
   For example, common "*law*" and case
"*law*" alike has held that accessories to
crimes can either be:
   A) Accountable with the crime;
   B) Negligent of the crime;
   C) Both of the above;
   D) But there is no D, "none of the
above."

What's gamed in court;
is forced onto the streets.   83   *What's proven in PASS;*
is proven on the streets.

But to those holding themselves
above the common "*law*" and case "*law*"
alike it's upheld that accessories to
their crimes can either:
A) Victimize their victim until they
are silent;
B) Victimize their victim unless he
still speaks out but then it's magically
a Civil case, not a criminal case;
C) Both of the above but the
victimized victim does not survive and
those holding themselves above the '*law*'
still gain pay <u>and</u> power regardless;
D) There is or isn't a D, "*none of
the above.*"

I for one am not going to just sit
around in slothful negligence being a
prideful witting accomplice to self-
evident Civil Rights abuse and obvious
inhumane treatment.
I am not going to them legitimately
cursing this great land of ours. Legitimately cursing helplessly dependent
civilians, innocent young children and
valuable institutions alike to death.
While having the audacity to call this
"*justice.*"

What's gamed in court;
is forced onto the streets.   84   *What's proven in PASS;*
is proven on the streets.

Why should everyone else pay <u>and</u> suffer for their disordering?

Why not consider everyone paying and potentially suffering from the same equally?

Seems to me that if we were all aligned in agreement, if we were all on the same page, then this wouldn't even be an issue today.

Why not consider being all on the same page?

I aim to be a good steward of taking back what's been stolen.

Why not own your own property?

I feel fortunate to have been blessed with the gifted seeds of great-ness. Great American seeds. Seeds now considered weeds for exclusive ulterior motives. And I won't turn my back on that. I will face the accused like I am supposed to.

Why not do things right?

Just because judges and attorneys aren't vigilant enough to grow good seeds and raise them right does not mean that the rest of us should have to suffer underneath the choking confines of being their weed.

Why not consider moms and dads of equal weight as judges or attorney's when it comes to growing their own children?

I believe that all people are still created equal. I know that ruling people aren't really exclusive.

Why not level the playing field and see eye-to-eye?

So, to fight corrupting and to pro- tect humanity, to hold the world to high- er standards with healing solutions I have Scientifically Convicted the lot of judges and lawyers with having overthrown the United States of America governments, juries, Democracies, everything and everyone.

Why not claim our rightful place on "top?"

Judges and attorneys have now been Scientifically Convicted of upholding and practicing a Conspiracy against Civil Rights in violation of Illinois State Statute 725 ILCS 5/8-21, Conspiracy to Commit Theft by deception in violation of

720 ILCS 5/8-2 and 720 ILCS 5/16-1, a
Conspiracy against universal Humanity in
violation Upright USA's Laws of
Leveraging Order, a Conspiracy against
universal Sanity in violation of the
Family Matters Mission, and a Conspiracy
to Misprision of Treason in violation of
720 ILCS 5/8-2 and 720 ILCS 5/30-2.

Bar associated judges and attorneys
have been Scientifically Convicted of
being Accountable with, and Negligent of
Civil Rights victimization's, inhumane
treatment victimization's, State Constitutional Rights victimization's, and
United States Constitution victimization's in direct violation of their own
sworn duty and responsibilities.

Judges and attorneys have been
Scientifically Convicted of Ruling by
Dictator Intimidation, Dictative Order
and leading with extortive and
exploitative Leverage against helplessly
dependent civilians.

Judges and attorneys have been
Scientifically Convicted of waging war on
the American People. As positioning
themselves as an enemy in the War on
Terrorism. With police officers and
civilians alike both DP-ed (Delusionally
Paradoxed)in the War on Drugs. And with
weighting the Rules of Engagement with an
automatic Motor of Mass Destruction

What's gamed in court;
is forced onto the streets.   87   *What's proven in PASS;*
is proven on the streets.

(MMD.) (See "The MMD Report" of a new Scientific discovery and new Law of Science.)

Judges and attorneys have been Scientifically Convicted of upholding and practicing a foreign and alienating war within the People with an excluding licensed umbrella over everything and everyone on the order, with same cause and effects, as Terrorism. Terrorism of the highest order.

Why not consider Scientific Standards and Disordering Standards equally?

Judges and attorneys have been Scientifically Convicted of overriding and undermining legitimate order to cause ill psychological defects on the order, cause and effects of brainwashing.

"The issue here isn't whether every student is brainwashed, it's whether it is appropriate."
- David Horowitz

Children bigger than others have been known to push helpless children down in order to take away something(s) that they want. This is on the order, cause

What's gamed in court;
is forced onto the streets.   88   What's proven in PASS;
is proven on the streets.

and effects of theft by and for bullyism.

Spiritual and psychological "*bullyism*" is no different than physical bullyism. But it is worse. Because it leaves
the victims only able to take the pain
and suffering out on themselves or those
that they are close to. They can't fight
back against what's bigger than them or
against what they don't know. And they
especially can't fight back against
something that isn't even usable to them.

Since the days of Adam and Eve
tricksters/slicksters/devils/deceivers/
bullies/snakes/scorpions have always
instigating the unassuming and then
manipulated them. Pushed them down and
then took something away. Scared them and
then "*protected.*" Baited and then
switched. Hedged then Leveraged. Brokered
and then vised. Undermined and then
overridden. All disordering "*authori-
zations*" in order to physically and
psychologically take something away from
its rightful owner.

Why not support bullies and their
victims equally?

Psychological bullies are no
different than physical bullies in that
they take advantage of weak and
unassuming victims, even of weakened

victims that they've created, by setting them up to fail. And then victimizing them when they do fail. Reaping some premeditated reward when their victims can't protect themselves. Or can't know any better.

This began, and still is, on the Order, cause and effects of the Devil.

A Scientific Conviction that this lineage, or this mindset if you will, is the children of Satan.

In court it's much much worse though. Because it's absolute, officer enforced and officially encouraged. Especially if by simple Neglect.

It's ordering victims disordered so that they'll be easily taken advantage of. It's on the Order, cause and effects of a Satanic Conspiracy.

The Satanic Conspiracy is those who think and act, even enforce in unison by and for the Devil's brand of thinking.

Adult children of a like-mind to their fatherly Devil *"authorize"* themselves illegitimate order(s) to take advantage of good and legitimate order. That's what they do. That's all they know.

The message, or *"law"* if you will, is that you have to trick people. You have to bait and switch simply to follow the law.

The absolute LAW is to be a bully and a "*bully*" or else you are a Criminal and a "*criminal*." If you're not you can and will be found guilty and "*guilty*" in a court of "*law*" (Hidden Leverage.)

Otherwise, if you aren't bully-minded and bully-bodied then they think you deserve to be locked up. And to lose everything you own and every relation-ship you had. Either be like them or you'll be forced into being like them.

It's like a judge told me, "What choice do you have?"

What choice do I have? They pressure and even trick people into being one way, and then punish us for being that way.

That's worse than entrapment! It's like an automatic Death Trap!

After time, trial and vestment, those who become accustom to this counterintuitive-ism must develop what I call the Parasitic Effect.

The Parasitic Effect is caused by Authorization Disorder. Where they take what they want regardless.

They only have to benefit the sameness of their authorizers. Regardless of who or what has to pay for it. And regardless of whom else has to suffer for it.

After physical attachments parasites have no conscious of their hosts except

What's gamed in court;
is forced onto the streets.
91
What's proven in PASS;
is proven on the streets.

taking that which they want.

Once the hunt is over nothing else matters except feeding their own wants and desires.

While their host is often incapacitated and bleeding out.

Psychologically speaking, this is on the order, cause and effects of Psychotic Insanity.

The Scientific Discovery of the Law of Leverage Disorder has its self Scientifically Convicted (the highest standard known to mankind) that judges overriding plus attorney's undermining Authorization Disorder(s) absolutely cause ill psychological effects and ill physical defects due to prescribing compulsive divisions.

Due to Authorization Disorder and it's Parasitic Effects Scientific Convictions must obviously prevail. As only they can in the end anyway.

Scientific Convictions are also higher standards with healing solutions.

"Patriotism is easy to understand in America; it means looking out for your-self by looking out for your country."
- Calvin Coolidge

What's gamed in court;
is forced onto the streets.   92   *What's proven in PASS;*
is proven on the streets.

"A man's country is not a certain area of land, of mountains, rivers, and woods, but it is a principle; and patriotism is loyalty to that principle."
   - *George Williams Curtis*

"Where liberty dwells, there is my country."
   - *Benjamin Franklin*

"A good scientist is a person with original ideas. A good engineer is a person who makes a design that works with as few original ideas as possible. There are no prima donnas in engineering."
   - *Freeman Dyson*

"As an engineer I'm constantly spotting problems and plotting how to solve them."
   - *James Dyson*

"I'm an engineer, but what I find important and necessary is that you just learn things as you go along."
   - *Terrence Howard*

"The world is a dangerous place to

What's gamed in court;
is forced onto the streets.   93   *What's proven in PASS;*
is proven on the streets.

live; not because of the people who are evil, but because of the people who don't do anything about it."
    - *Albert Einstein*

"Always do right. This will gratify some people and astonish the rest."
    - *Mark Twain*

"The weak can never forgive. Forgiveness is an attribute of the strong."
    - *Mahatma Gandi*

"Learn from yesterday, live for today, hope for tomorrow. The important thing is not to stop questioning."
    - *Albert Einstein*

What's gamed in court;
is forced onto the streets.   94   *What's proven in PASS;*
is proven on the streets.

Be true and accept developing the truth my dear friends. And together we'll bury both corrupting and hurting with both progress and healing.

The Law Doctor

5. Mental cancer - The MMD Report

{A Scientific Judicial & Scientific
Psychological Discovery.}

Some jobs blow other people's lives out of proportion. While the only thing truly out of proportion are some jobs themselves.

The Motor of Mass Destruction (MMD) theory has now proven to be a scientific fact.

Question everything and refresh everything!

MMD is a new Law of Science that is Human Debilitating Kinetic effects due to Static System Dynamics.

Recognize the impossible.

What's gamed in court;
is forced onto the streets.   97   *What's proven in PASS;*
is proven on the streets.

Compulsively Kinetic side effects are where Superstatic Dynamics meets regular free will.

The impossible cannot be saved.

The scientific, psychology and physiology study that was used to research for this book has proven that courtroom weegie-like vicing plus vising can be accurately depicted as an automatic machine (see the 3CCD paradigm graph) inherently consuming all aspects of life.

Save only the possible.

Be the most responsible.

It is well known that theirs is a like-minded, enterprising solidarity ring ruling over people, the People, the police, all other practices, all other professionals, and all other policies alike with well-known debilitating side effects.

Debilitating side effects that can now be accurately understood as a perpetual drain on humanity.

Draining side effects that can and will damage all aspects of financial, mental and physical well-being. Just like a well-oiled machine.

What's gamed in court;
is forced onto the streets.   98   *What's proven in PASS;*
is proven on the streets.

It is also well known that those operating the MMD can and will protect the MMD first and foremost and above all. Better minds can and will be torn to shreds with mental "*handicaps*" to posture the solidarity ring protecting the machine if and when necessary.

These potentially traumatizing "*handicaps*" are then enforced as absolute LAW.

Side effects from these are designed to be reinforced permanent, perpetual, irreversible and irreparable.

These facts have been studied, researched and verified.

These facts can be legitimately (unexpectedly) tested.

The Scientific Method used in this report is irrefutable. It is the highest standard of accuracy.

The Motor of Mass Destruction (MMD) is a true Law of Science.

Inside this book you find out why we are all subjects to other practice's pride binding us to lower standards enforced and harmful "*solutions*" empowered just to keep the MMD running smoothly.

But this machine is being mechanized to consume the world's humanity all on its own.

In reality, laws and policies aren't

What's gamed in court;
is forced onto the streets.   99   *What's proven in PASS;*
is proven on the streets.

even needed anymore to keep the beast fed.

The MMD can run all on its own.

Its "*victims*" don't even have to exist.

Its victimized victims are all that have to be real in order to be taken advantage of.

3CCD GRAPH OF THE CANCER CAUSING MMD

WELCOME to the world of MMD. In reality, it's a land of make believe except for the side effects.

BEWARE! It is a land of figurative *"make believe"* and literal MAKE BELIEVE! It has to be. Because it is an impossible system!

(3CCD means three Concurrent Complex Dimensions.)

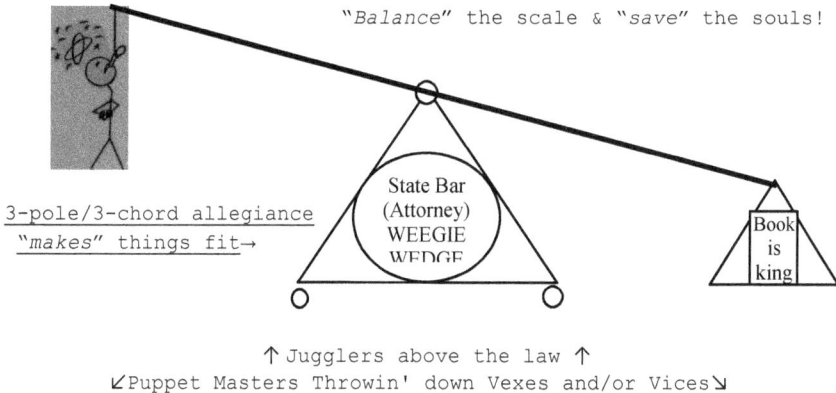

"Balance" the scale & *"save"* the souls!

3-pole/3-chord allegiance
"makes" things fit→

State Bar
(Attorney)
WEEGIE
WEDGE

Book
is
king

↑ Jugglers above the law ↑
↙Puppet Masters Throwin' down Vexes and/or Vices↘

HUMAN SIDE	INHUMAN SIDE
(Intentionally Degenerative Side)	(Intentionally Generative Side)
—Confusions like *"innocent"*	Amplified supportive Labels +
—All implications = wrong	All implications = right +

What's gamed in court;
is forced onto the streets.

What's proven in PASS;
is proven on the
streets.

The Law Doctor

—Degrading posture & positions	Upgrading postures & positions +
— Degrading treatment	Upgrading treatment +
_ Dehumanizing conditioning	Idolizing conditioning +
_ Maddening/numbing cells	Prestigious business as usual +
_ Inhumane, punishing *"process"*	Gloating, superior-ating press +
_ Probation's espionage	Probation's vested compliance +
_ Probation's sabotage	Probation's liable allegiance +
_ Psychiatrist's espionage	Psychiatrist's vested compliance +
_ Psychiatrist's sabotage	Psychiatrist's liable allegiance +
_ Jailer's espionage	Jailer's vested compliance +
_ Jailer's sabotage	Jailer's liable allegiance +
_ County nurse espionage	County nurse vested compliance +
_ County nurse sabotage	County nurse liable allegiance +
_ County doctor espionage	County doctor vested compliance +
_ County doctor sabotage	County doctor liable allegiance +
_ Common English obstructed	Foreign language leveraged +
_ Alienating mechanics degenerate	Mechanics generate +
_ Demoralized or impossible will	Upgraded will +
- Demoralized or impossible posture	Upgraded posture +
_ Demoralized or impossible position	Upgraded position +
_ No Bill of Rights paid	Whatever *"Justice"* submits victim +

What's gamed in court;
is forced onto the streets.
streets.

102

What's proven in PASS;
is proven on the

— No enforcements ensure Bills are paid

Enforcements ensure that Bills are not paid   +

The compulsive score/feelings enforced:

-24      **+24**

(Wish I were a book or a joke!?)
Do you see the now vested, liable and therefore unspeakable trends? And where they naturally tend to take all of us?
Right here is where it takes all of us except those above it:

As is, there is no getting out of the inherent traps on both sides. We're all trapped in too deep with those above us compulsively violating us.
The result for one side is chasin' ghosts while neglecting the inevitable.

What's gamed in court;
is forced onto the streets.   103   *What's proven in PASS;*
is proven on the
streets.

Because one of the forever flaws in the "*law*" is that the left side can never equal the right side. (As death can never equal life.)

The two sides can only permanently and perpetually deviate more and more and more forever and ever.

And you see this played out in real life.

For example, if an inmate commits suicide in a jail cell do they ease up on inhumane treatments, or do they increase the inhumane treatments? Do they consider their victims emotions, or do they buy security cameras?

Quilt & "*quilt*" is almost mandatory by presence alone. As is "*fixing*" the systems just to keep them as is. "*More*" and More of the same.

The net result is that the left side is guilty and/or "*guilty*" by non-association alone. And this trend goes as far and as wide as the rulers need it to.

The bigger crimes are that this system is absolutely harmful for one side regardless, and absolutely corrupting for the other side regardless. This is what's known as the Duel Death Spiral (DDS.)

What scientists call the point of no return in an outer space vortex hole and the likes, is the event horizon. That's point of no return where no life that

What's gamed in court;
is forced onto the streets.   104   *What's proven in PASS;*
streets.   *is proven on the*

enters into it that can ever escape again. Not even light itself. Not even knowledge.

In courts that point of no return was crossed for us all back when superior *"freedom of the press"* reports suppressingly became almost invincible ruling over permanently and perpetually inferior-ating Free Speech.

Back when superiors could start putting words in the *"mouths"* of helplessly dependent inferiors on formal report form evidence.

Yes, when *"whatever"* on a formal report evidence with the superior witness began trumping and/or violating even the truth of inferior-ated Free Speech victims.

Why not consider that fudging the reports of those whose lives are dependent on your jobs could actually affect their lives in reality?

The MMD Vortex only spins faster and faster until complete decay. And it cannot stop as is.

Analytically, the effects are much greater than two times an exponential equation. Especially when digital *"cover"* and *"protection"* in order to **COVER IT ALL UP** is compulsively ordered easily from detached vantage positions.

And especially since only the most victimized victims can suffer the consequences from it.

And/or suffer worse for speaking out about it.

The MMD causes mental cancer.

Mental cancer causes not only more mental cancer, but financial cancer and physical cancer as well.

What's gamed in court;
is forced onto the streets.
streets.

106

What's proven in PASS;
is proven on the

The 3CUCD (Three Compulsively United Complex Dividing) Wedge

{Also known as the manufacturer of enmity.}

This is ENMITY. The ideal idol of enmity manufacturing. A compulsive Weegie Wedging, absolute dividing, back zapper.

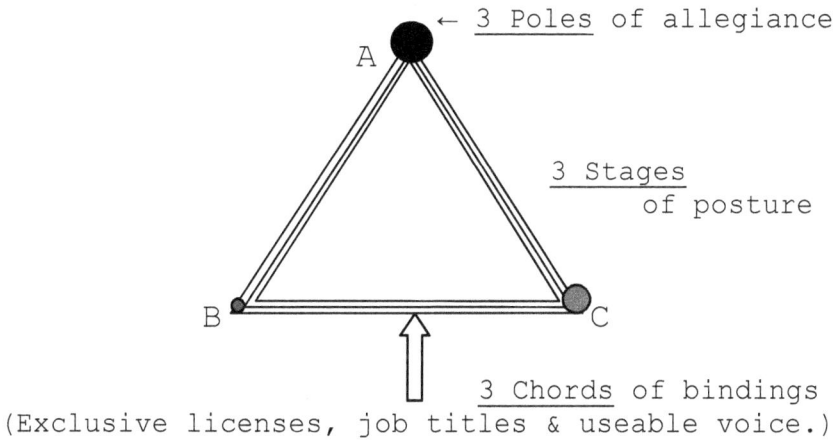

← 3 Poles of allegiance

3 Stages
of posture

3 Chords of bindings
(Exclusive licenses, job titles & useable voice.)

(3 Stages with 3 Poles and at least 3 Chords of allegiance obviously, self-evidently and self-provingly equals a shared consciousness.)

*What's gamed in court;
is forced onto the streets.*   107   *What's proven in PASS;
is proven on the
streets.*

Stage A. The highest force in the wedge
is the intimidating contrasting factor.
This force sits on the highest stage. It
carries the heaviest weight because it is
obviously implied visually, applied
vocally and/or mechanically via routine,
and is exploitatively coerced and
extortionately enforced. It's an enmity,
Bully and/or "*bully*" pulpit.

Stage B. The middle force in the wedge is
a contrary condemnation factor. This
opposing and alienating force has the
middle-weight factor because it must be
verbal, and can be reinforced with
inferiorating stars, guns, badges, etc.
Superiorating stars, guns, badges, etc.,
that are illegal for the other side to
show.

Stage C. The lightest, often negative,
force in the wedge. This attraction
force, absolutely with trickery, is a
little bit of "*protection*." It's a "*must
have*," else no real weight is given.
Without it this side obviously carries
even less weight. However, even this
light weight instinctively protects the
inhumane Weegie Wedging first and
foremost. It has to. Or else it doesn't
exist.

What's gamed in court;
is forced onto the streets.   108   *What's proven in PASS;*
streets.   *is proven on the*

Sanity and Humanity outside of the Weegie Wedging are simply an outcast. They are irrelevant.

Sanity and Humanity are obviously "*meant*" and Meant to be divided and conquered.

Humanity and sanity gets in the way of the excluding business.

Permanently and perpetually less humanity and sanity actually equals better business, more power and more profit.

In this 3CUCD Paradigm Scheme it's easy to see why outsider's Bill of Rights, free voice and free will must be eliminated by any means necessary and by all options available.

If this court were to pay their Bill of Rights then position A would not exist. Thus, that would reveal corruption. And thus, would have to admit humanity and sanity exists. And this whole Paradigm Scheme would then collapse.

Thus, their permanent and perpetual unconstitutional abridge that's being upheld with inhumane treatment would be a humane, well-traveled road instead.

But no Rights and no Humanity and no Sanity exists in their scheme of things.

Compulsively, no Rights and no humanity and no sanity are their RULE of things.

What's gamed in court;
is forced onto the streets.
streets.

110

What's proven in PASS;
is proven on the

The MMD Ignition Switch

<u>The three points of originally detached contacts that are now "*hot*" wired together</u> that began the MMD running are that People's Bill of Rights are exhausted not being paid freely (or even accepted for that matter), Free Speech is foreign and not applicable, and free will representation is alienating and unacceptable to the machine.

At worse, Rights, will and voice are opposed to at all costs to the same.

Rights, will and voice are inherently opposed to in favor of the MMD running instead. In favor of the highest machine in control.

Which spreads because it's enforced to be illegal not to, below the motor, and even beyond the motor. After all, this is the "*law.*"

What's gamed in court is enforced on the streets.

At best, Rights, will and voice cannot even be possibly considered by an unconscious machine.

The Law Doctor

What's gamed in court;
is forced onto the streets.
streets.

What's proven in PASS;
is proven on the

<u>The 3 Concurrent Complex Dimensions (3CCD) of domination</u> (3 Poles, 3 Chords & 3 Stages) are super-reinforced with even "*professional*" encouragement and "*public*" enforcement as need be to keep the MMD running.

The starter and driver combination of the above initiates and then maintains the MMD while debilitating humanity without effort.

Human Beings are simply gravity-fed, flowing fuel consumed to keep the motor running.

While tax dollars keep the power on.

What's gamed in court;
is forced onto the streets.
streets.

113

What's proven in PASS;
is proven on the

The Law Doctor

What's gamed in court;
is forced onto the streets.
114
streets.

What's proven in PASS;
is proven on the

Psychological & Physiological Effects from the MMD

From a psychological and physiological perspective, the downward cycle is like a perpetual drain. A perpetually draining "*process*" that is easier to accept falling deeper and deeper into than it is (**Impossible)** to swim your way out of.

The deeper one slides down into the drain the harder the "*pressures*" and (**Pressures)** of its figurative vices and literal vises become if and when the MMD is opposed. (See the Chapter on Thinking in 3-CCDD for the meaning of this new nomenclature regarding "parenthesis," *italics*, brackets and **BOLD** fonts and divisions.)

Absolutely weighted vices vise to play and pressure games with our emotions, money, children, rights, responsibilities, freedom, elderly care, health, voice, safety and sanity until submission to it.

Without so much as a search for evidence, especially only with premeditated fear, this inhumane drain can and will be used against its victims regardless.

It's easily manipulated. And anyone baited or brought into this machine can and will be victimized.

What's gamed in court;
is forced onto the streets.
streets.

116

What's proven in PASS;
is proven on the

Overall

Overall, the Static Dynamics from this motor is bad for everyone.

Unfortunately we are all trapped in one way or another to its vexes and/or its vises.

However, no sane mind should be exposed to the MMD. If OSHA wasn't tied under it then they would probably outlaw it.

Likewise for the military, FBI, CIA, etc. They're all tied underneath of it and can't even stand up to confront it.

As a result, the suppression and/or lasting trauma of being exposed to the MMD, or "*scales*" of "*justice*," as some may proclaim, is now indisputable.

It's Weegie Magic!

It's obvious, self-evident and especially self-proving that there are differential shock rates per individual that causes trauma. A formula based on intellect.

For example, could you imagine going from the highest point in life, the highest paid position, highest prestige, highest authorizing posture in life, all the way down to the bottom of the bottom?

That would be variably traumatizing

per individual based on the subject's own
intellect.

What's gamed in court;
is forced onto the streets.   118
streets.

What's proven in PASS;
is proven on the

Need Help?

If you need more help understanding
the fact that the MMD is a Scientific Law
bound to debilitating humanity and
sanity, then just answer the following
questions yourself.

What's best for their business?

1) Life or death?
2) Healthy or disabled?
3) Sane or insane?
4) Parents or no parents?
5) Joy or sadness?
6) Morals or no morals?
7) Constitution or no constitution?

Now, for the second part of this
quiz, go back through the above list of
questions and ask yourself what is better
for life, our society and our economy?

Not only is the MMD an absolute Law
of Science, but it should be obvious. It
can be tested.
The MMD is inversely proportional to
life, to humanity and to sanity.

It's a human eating machine!

This inverse relationship between

What's gamed in court;
is forced onto the streets.   119   *What's proven in PASS;*
is proven on the
streets.

all aspects of life and death can only grow farther and farther apart all of the time and forever as is.

Not only is the MMD a handicap creator, but it's a handicap enforcer.

We are dead under it!

The Cumulative Results

The cumulative results of the MMD running over society by passing everything through it is a permanent and perpetual drain.

Once you enter into it today there is no coming out of it. And it doesn't matter if you were put into it legitimately or illegitimately.

For each and every person, especially the innocent and unassuming, that approaches the weak and human side of the MMD (the fuel side) they will just burn right through the cylinder. That's the "*process*."

For each and every innocent and presumptive victim that blows through the strong and inhuman side of the MMD (the air intake) they will just flow through the cylinder.

Both the fuel and the air intakes are governed by the State Bar's Weegie Wedge. Ensuring that the fuel and the air burn effectively only for them.

What's gamed in court;
is forced onto the streets.
streets.

121

What's proven in PASS;
is proven on the

The Law Doctor

What's gamed in court;
is forced onto the streets.
streets.

What's proven in PASS;
is proven on the

System Upgrades

When they need to upgrade their motor they easily petition or join legislators for more throttle control. The more that they modify society and the economy the better their performance.

Air intake can simply be tweaked with better badges or bigger guns. That's not hard to modify.

But adjusting the fuel is a little craftier. You have to have its pulse, plant seeds of leverage, and then nurture them into the catalyst you want them to be.

Adjusting the fuel is like growing a seed. It takes time, nurture and the correct conditions.

Adjusting the air intake is easy. It often just takes the sameness of hot air to excite it.

Given known human instincts, they can actually turbo-charge the air intake very easily.

Once the system is upgraded however, there is no going back. It's like modifying a cylinder head.

Once you grind off the metal then you can't just put it the metal back. And if you take off too much, then you've taken off to much and the motor is ruined.

Likewise, if you turbo-charge the air in a humans mind nurturing them fully vested, vexed and/or vised, then you can't just take it away.

What's gamed in court;
is forced onto the streets.
streets.

124

What's proven in PASS;
is proven on the

The Perpetually Bad Vortex Today

The motor today is running badly. There are many side effects to the vices that are needed to keep the drain covered to keep the MMD running.

But once the drain gets bigger than the vices covering it up, well, then it runs bad for a while. It starts to wobble. It's like a broken washing machine. It gets out of balance and can only wobble more and more until you either fix it or get a new one.

Or, it's like a tire that wears itself out of balance. It wobbles worse and worse and worse until you get a new one. One way or another.

Mentally, the Static Dynamics of the MMD are obviously an absolute bipolar force to everyone involved. This is obvious, self-evident and self-provable because of the fact that each person involved must consider at the same time two intense perspectives towards two opposing directions upon their most vested objects.

Pride in the eye is blinding.

Hence, the "*best*" bipolar personality is the best at this.

Additionally, considering the actual authority of inhumane mechanics and state statutes needed to excuse inherent pain and sufferance, this adds a sociopathic aspect to the MMD.

Enforced public psychosis from the system should be obvious.

And the only real defense is to be aware of fire starters.

Recognizers of the impossible BEWARE!

The impossible dynamics of this motor aggravates the more knowledgeable. Those of us who see and feel it much like a giant bug zapper zapping unsuspecting bugs that are tricked into flying into it.

Especially when we bugs simply stand on the truth. In which we are then "*forced*" and Forced into it.

The State Bar's three chord bindings plus three physical stages with three poles of allegiance with exploitive psychological and/or extortive physical back-ups now vexed and/or vised in on their side of things actually ensures that "*bugs*" who enter near to the heart of the MMD Paradigm Scheme are **SQUASHED** with no Rights, no Will and no Voice at all. (Save "*accepting*" servanthood.)

Thus, humanity and sanity are mentally bound and/or else physically bound. With additional demoralizing, dehumanizing and sanity deteriorating conditioning available for exercise to protect inhumanity over humanity.

Any sane or humane intervention attempt to help balance the MMD can and will be a spark to get the MMD "*modified*" and/or Modified to keep it running and everyone else as fuel or turbo-charged air.

The Static Dynamics are that the MMD operates to cause and/or perpetuate many mental, physical, financial and well-being disorders. Disorders that are irreversible and irreparable.

The symptoms from MMD are obviously chronic. They are illegal not to be.

The cause of these chronic diseases are obvious, self-evident and even self-provable.

What's gamed in court;
is forced onto the streets.
streets.

128

What's proven in PASS;
is proven on the

Dictated Status

So, the dictated status quote is to either accept the needlessly wasteful cost, pain and suffering or else you will be harmed even more.

Accept that you have no Bill of Rights owed to you or else you will be harmed even more.

Accept that you will be treated inhumanely or else you will be punished even more.

You either accept that you have no free will or else you will be tortured like you don't.

What's gamed in court;
is forced onto the streets.
streets.

129

What's proven in PASS;
is proven on the

The Law Doctor

What's gamed in court;
is forced onto the streets.
streets.

130

What's proven in PASS;
is proven on the

Status Quote

But this is nothing new. This is the way that it has always been.

People in power get use to the power and then get carried away with their power until the little guys finally realize, "hey, we're just getting wasted, used and abused here!"

This has always been the problem with growing mountains of Dictatorships instead of holding back, doing things the right way, and letting Democracies be level, eye-to-eye, upfront and equal.

This is nothing new. Just new titles and new angles.

But any and all Dictatorships are obviously impossible.

Yeah, they may start out fine. But when problems arise, and they always do, it's only the little people who can legally suffer. Therein lays the perpetual drain on society.

An entire area minus one, trying to serve the one, can only last for so long.

Until one day it gets to the point where you either accept allegiance to whatever the one wants, or else you lose everything and everyone until you give in to it.

Granted, today is a much more complicated Dictatorship. ("*Kudos*" to the

What's gamed in court;
is forced onto the streets.

131

What's proven in PASS;
is proven on the
streets.

Bar for that one!)   But the end
results are still the same. You either go
along with it or it murders you.

It's just spread out across the
board now instead of outright murder.
Which actually has more and greater
consequences.

America's Dictators are the figurative *"worse"* and the literal Worse that
the world has ever known.

That's a fact.

Not only can innocent people be held
liable for other people's mistakes, they
can and will be held liable for other
people's delusions, or even gossip, until
we cave in and accept responsibility for
their mistakes. And we can and will be
punished for the impossibilities of
systems. Which amplifies the compulsive
punishments automatically depending on
how many systems you are subject to and
how many impossible contradictions that
those systems have to each other.

All at tax payers more than double
exponentially wasted expense.

Which is just like sucking money
into someone else's vacuum cleaner while
flushing our children's lives down the
toilet.

What's gamed in court;
is forced onto the streets.

What's proven in PASS;
is proven on the
streets.

They can railroad, ruin and run-around without conscious today.

If nothing else, just to save face at the smaller people's expense.

The unspeakable consequences on their helplessly dependent victims are the same.

But is this Equal Protection for all? Or crafty Obstruction of all?

Or is this just Animals and "crazy" animals?

When animals learn how to cut and prep heads off of other animals to hang on the wall, then pictures alone may never again suffice.

Obviously, animals are considered better than humans by "law."

Animals cannot possibly suffer like human beings can.

Without our Rights, will and voice, people and the People are obviously enslaved to other bigger people's voice and will.

Today we are all paying taxes and suffering the consequences to be prisoners of other people's pride.

The Law Doctor

What's gamed in court;
is forced onto the streets.
streets.

134

What's proven in PASS;
is proven on the

The Law Doctor

Truth P.O.W.'s in America:

Why's it my fault that I was born
with RIGHTS?
Why's it my fault that they were all
swiped?

Why's it my fault that Amendments
aren't added?
Why's it my fault that it's
impossible for all of us to stay in
order?
Instead of being free;
For what together we all could have
known?

Why's it my fault that Lassie gets
petted?
Why's it my fault that I get vetted?
Why's it my fault that sanity can't
comprehend the business of disorder?
Why's it my fault that I go to jail
for another mixed order?
Instead of being free;
For what together we all could have
said?

Why's it my fault that I'm forced to
be tongue tied?
Why's it my fault that free will is
just along for their ride?

What's gamed in court;
is forced onto the streets.
135
What's proven in PASS;
is proven on the
streets.

The Law Doctor

I'd build a bridge and cover the
gap;
But they deny to even let error be
shown;

I'd draw them a line and show them
the way;
But they deny that they are too far
gone;

From a child on they swore that we
could trust our RIGHTS;
But like our voice and will, they
get all tied up under their device;

And when the rubber meets the road;
Diversions and excuses are all that
we are told;

Owed Due Process was just a dream;
Bound servants are the real thing.

What's gamed in court;
is forced onto the streets.
streets.

136

What's proven in PASS;
is proven on the

The Law Doctor

Why should I have to move abroad,
become their citizen, and then sneak back
in just to get a little Due attention?
 The effects of little spells with
inherent vices and/or vises can't just
magically heal themselves;
 Their exclusive "*nexus*" and/or Nexus
holds us apart so tight;
 So it's impossible to unite, to
think or to even to be upright;

 How much worse will it all get for
the next generation?
 Maybe neglect should just turn
schools into wards and cut out all of the
middlemen?

 It sure beats bleeding young wills,
binding their souls and hurting young
hearts;
 Just because it makes a good
business plan.

 Why from childhood on;
 Would authorities let us be set up
to fail?

 Now either pay their "*buddies*" their
dues;
 Or else risk going to jail.

What's gamed in court;
is forced onto the streets.
streets.

What's proven in PASS;
is proven on the

The Law Doctor

All I ever dreamed about;
Was being a part of that place I
learned about in school;
But I stumbled through the dark
instead;
Made to feel, look and be treated
like a fool.

Maybe I should just get over it?
It's really no different than
Russian Roulette.

Why's it my fault that error got in
control?
Why's it my fault that neglect keeps
the status quote?

It's not my fault that I'm an
American P.O.W. in America;
Where the truth is the only thing
left that's "*worse*" than crime;

Where the weak is the only thing
"*criminal*" just because it is not strong;
Why's it my fault that humility is
dying as the last true American?

Why's it only my fault that
something is obviously wrong?
Why's it only my fault that they
made me not strong?

What's gamed in court;
is forced onto the streets.   138   *What's proven in PASS;*
streets.   *is proven on the*

<u>Tightening the Rope to Pull Start the Motor</u>

Over time and tricks, our Bill of RIGHTS, humane treatments and sane conditioning have all been both tricked out and trickled away.

Probably for a greater market share and for the ease of taking advantage of the already taken advantage of people.

It is self-evident what group of professionals have not only the motive and the opportunities to deplete the People. But who absolutely must deplete the People or else thing that they've ever worked for will be exposed as fraud and flushed down the drain.

And since it is known that there is no good science or true Laws practiced in their performance of court and its counsel then theirs has had to become a perpetually increasing deceptive practice just to cover it all up while appeasing all of the heartache and abuse caused.

The accelerating-only MMD is the result. And with it, the scientifically proven human debilitating kinetic dynamics by & for its static dynamics.

For example, how is it even possible that delusionally judging 3rd or 4th-hand between the "*best*" of two 2nd-hand false witness bearers could ever be right?

It can't.

That's like trying to catch fish off of a parking lot.

It's ludicrous.

But they are all deadly sins.

And it's the ones who aren't even doing the sinning who are paying the price for the sinning and suffering the consequences from the sinning.

If anything, there should be a law against mindless practices running over humanity and against deceptive practices ruling over ruining everything.

Personal Perspective of a Truth Attorney vs. the MMD

From a personal perspective, I can never again in good faith, good consciousness or good will license myself under the unfaithful, unconscious and bad will MMD. Because if I did then that would be evidence that I accept allegiance to a figurative and/or literal beast.

The Law Doctor

What's gamed in court;
is forced onto the streets.
streets.

142

What's proven in PASS;
is proven on the

Patriotic Perspective of a Truth Attorney vs. the MMD

From a patriotic perspective, I can never again neglect MMD in place of We the People. That's just sociopathic. Not to mention treason. Not to mention inhumane. Not to mention insane.

The Law Doctor

What's gamed in court;
is forced onto the streets.
streets.

144

What's proven in PASS;
is proven on the

The Law Doctor

<u>Maybe Motorized Walls Built Crooked just
    to Divide us that Way Should Fall?</u>

    Why shouldn't the walls of error
fall?
    I mean they waste billions on quick
sand to "*hold it up*" anyway;

    Why shouldn't the masterhood of
falsehood reveals its holes?
    I mean their Jrunk Judicial Drivers
that guide us are not sane;

    A True Democracy jury;
    Now there's our American way;

    The Dictators power was really none;
    Maybe I'll straighten it up today;

    Or maybe I should just look away?
    Let it all turn into dust?

    But if I did then loosing America
would absolutely be my fault;
    So maybe I'll muster up some salt?

    Maybe I'll take my RIGHTS & will &
voice;
    And then own all over this place?

What's gamed in court;
is forced onto the streets.   145
streets.

What's proven in PASS;
    is proven on the

The Law Doctor

Maybe I'll fight the good fight;
And start a brand new race;

Maybe that's what I owe those souls;
Those souls who gifted me with this
place;

So I guess that the only question
now is;
Which side of the wall will you be
on when it falls?

Which side will you be on when our
children remember when?
Maybe going out on top is the only
answer then?

It could go either way you know;
Our vested People or "*their*" little
men;

From this concentration camp on;
There's only one thing that matters;

Serving my Lord like a real man;
Cause all others just seem to
flatter me in;

But silver scales are known to have
silver tongues;
Why anyone would choose them over
God, was the wrong "*answer*" then.

What's gamed in court;   *What's proven in PASS;*
is forced onto the streets.   146   *is proven on the*
streets.

The Law Doctor

So I'll stick to the truth;
Because only it can keep control;

All others can go by the wayside;
Like chafe blowing down the road;

It's futile to hold on to error;
And watch our country go;

So let's get a grip;
And shake those demons out of
control.

What's gamed in court;
is forced onto the streets.   147   *What's proven in PASS;*
streets.   *is proven on the*

The Law Doctor

What's gamed in court;
is forced onto the streets.
streets.

148

What's proven in PASS;
is proven on the

Certified American

NOW, uniting and/or strengthening
bonds with LOVE, COURAGE, FAITH, JOY,
STRENGTH, by and for but through our
Founding Fathers, the way, the truth, the
light, now there's where we need to
squat.

Being a Certified American by and
for the Upright USA Race Family Matters
Mission, is a whole other direction than
the old status quote. With completely
opposite considerations.

What's gamed in court;
is forced onto the streets.
streets.

149

What's proven in PASS;
is proven on the

The Law Doctor

What's gamed in court;
is forced onto the streets.
streets.

150

What's proven in PASS;
is proven on the

Constitutional Perspectives of a Truth Attorney vs. the MMD

From a United States Constitution perspective, the MMD is enforced and/or persuaded anti-constitution. It's a traitor by nature. It's a shooting traitor by actions. It's a potentially explosive traitor by neglect.

Those who protect this device and its inherent vices and vises over real live human beings, well, they're obviously its children.

The initial vice with not bowing down to this allegiance is that civilians can and will be gagged and demoted both mentally and physically at least if that's what it takes.

Gagged and demoted with no RIGHTS, no will and no level voice.

Victims can and will be harmed even worse if they maintain their Bill of RIGHTS, level voice, free will and officials RESPONSIBILITY to them all.

Yet, these are basic human needs. Basic needs that you can and will go to jail for having. (Being human and all.)

The sustaining vise is that careers are fully vested in protecting inhumanity over humanity. And actually worse than that is that inhumanity is rendering humanity null, void and/or *"worse."*

Inhumanity is ordering humanity to be like it. But, obviously so can't. So humanity is *"criminal"* until it can. Or, a loose-loose authority.

So pride in their careers alone is will, motive and opportunity enough to keep the MMD running in place and ruining in other places.

What's gamed in court;
is forced onto the streets.
streets.

152

What's proven in PASS;
is proven on the

The Lost Keys To The Weegie Magic Wedging Machine

The key to the Bar's "*success*" [***SUPPRESSION* AND/OR *TRAUMATIZATION***] in their decision making enterprise and all of its inherent vexes and/or vises is that their group dynamics have three stages of demoralization over people and The People. An implied and/or enforced intimidation factor ruling over a factory of sameness, and an "*attraction*" factor ruling over a factory of sameness to keep people and/or The People hooked.

And like the Devil, it's almost impossible to teach anyone else that these three prestigious looking "*professionals*" should not exist when they're right there in your face.

Especially when they "*own*" the best venue with automatic media support to do it in.

Thus, opposition is virtually and/or literally futile.

At best, opposition only hurts one's self.

At worse, opposition only hurts one's self even more in all ways possible.

Thus, join in on the permanent and perpetual drain on the United States of America, pay for it all and suffer from

What's gamed in court;
is forced onto the streets.   153   *What's proven in PASS;*
is proven on the
streets.

it all, or else be an outcast <u>plus</u> pay
for it all even more <u>and</u> suffer from it
all even more.

What's gamed in court;
is forced onto the streets.
streets.

154

What's proven in PASS;
is proven on the

Marked Keys

    Another key to the Bar's "*success*" is that any and all personal and professional license gifts them with final "*authority*" over those deciding matters in court.

    Which, unfortunately, is a monumental mistake handicapping the best professions and best minds and the best of intentions to then be upheld subject to the lowest of standards.

    This is a handicap of local, national and Biblical proportions.

The Law Doctor

What's gamed in court;
is forced onto the streets.
streets.

156

What's proven in PASS;
is proven on the

Is this the end?

Please, let Rights, Humanity &
Sanity reign.

It has to be.

From a personal, patriotic and moral
perspective I can never again conspire
with those obviously against the same.
And who themselves make themselves
impossible to follow.

Because if I did it would imply and
eventually mean that I accepted
allegiance to a degenerating deceptive
practice as final authority over me.

And I'm not selling my soul.

No matter what.

What's gamed in court;
is forced onto the streets.
streets.

157

What's proven in PASS;
is proven on the

The Law Doctor

What's gamed in court;
is forced onto the streets.
streets.

158

What's proven in PASS;
is proven on the

The Universal Conclusion

So, from an Engineers perspective, the MMD was designed to fail. As it has now been diagnosed to fail.

The prognosis is that financial, physical and psychological expenses will increase as Catastrophic failure is inevitable.

From a Judicial Scientists perspective, failure is at hand.

From a Scientific Psychiatrists perspective, healing is here.

From a Christian's perspective, the Kingdom of Heaven is in the other hand.

From a parent's perspective, the MMD is a trespassing and abusing machine on top of the most vulnerable children in the world.

The MMD not only prescribes Parental Alienation Syndromes (PAS) as Author Linda Gottlieb discovered, but Leverages it.

She acted appropriately to correct it trying to get the detaching courts to accept it. But they actually enforce PAS. So obviously they Neglected it. So they are liable for that too.

The MMD adulterates normal parenthood while harming the most vulnerable minds.

The MMD adulterates normal

executives while corrupting our most valuable institutions.

From a systems perspective, the MMD gags and/or binds to demote people, professions and the most valuable institutions in the world.

From a financial perspective, the MMD guarantees loss.

From a psychological perspective, the MMD guarantees disorder.

From a physiological perspective, the MMD guarantees degeneration.

From a government perspective, the MMD guarantees not only corruption, but corrupting.

And not only corrupting, but enforced corrupting.

And not only enforced corrupting, but Neglect of enforced corrupting.

From a Bar member's perspective, business is good and/or better.

And when business is good and/or better then brain laundering is business.

From a punishment and crime perspective, they're not even in the same ball park.

"*Well, just stay out of it,*" some might say.

But they forced it onto me.

One cannot live by their own Bill of RIGHTS and the Truth today and stay out of it. Taxes alone prove culpability.

And trying to live by the Truth is an automatic three strikes against you today if you are a Constitutional Christian Father.

From God's perspective, the MMD is a sin breeding machine.

The Laws of Science help us understand that the only possible side effects to sinful judging between two sinful false witness bearers is exponentially more and more sin.
Thus, the MMD is an automatic sin breeding machine that we're paying for.

It's an impossible system people! Please beware!

From a classical physicist's perspective, the 2nd Law (indisputable) of Thermal Dynamics proves that there is no escape from this systems decay compounded onto all of those people and things subject to it.

But, from an *I R Physics* perspective there is relief only in the Lord. The proprietary Kinetic Dynamics, Static Dynamics, Transfiguration, *I R Physics* and all of its derivatives owned by The Upright USA Race & Family Matters Mission has solutions.

"If anyone thirsts, let him come to Me (God's child) and drink.
"He who believes in Me (Jesus,) as the Scripture has said, out of his mind will flow rivers of living water." {John 7:37b & 38}

So please, let Rights, Humanity & Sanity (RHS) ring. Only then can the ultimate Truth prevail.
All for one & One for all.

This is now on us. His siblings. Those of us who are the chosen ones. Who stand in honor following His way. Refusing to bow down or even comply with error leaders.
We are His only hands and His only feet here on this dirt. It's time that somebody backs Him up.

"My doctrine is not Mine, but His who sent Me." {John 7:16}

Their motor is not only ruined, but it's ruining everything and everyone.

It's time for new life.
It's time to believe.
It's time to comply with life.
It's time to defy death.

Heavens Lawyers

Truth Attorney's. Truth attorney's represent the Way, the Truth and the Light.

The Upright USA Race and Family Matters Mission inherently enables Truth Attorney's. Truth Attorney's inherently unite and/or strengthening bonds of LOVE.

LOVE by and for but through Truth.

We promote Engineered Governments with Scientific Standards, Sane Principles, Humane Order, Human Authority, and Civilizing Rule, rules and rulers.

We develop a more precise society and economy, certify true Americans, license responsible authors, certify speakers, incubate legitimate representatives by and for all of the above.

Together, we'll resurrect the world as we now know it away from the Devil's inherently compulsive 21st Century Crucifixion.

It's time to believe.

It's time to live.

It's time to defy death.

The Law Doctor

What's gamed in court;
is forced onto the streets.
streets.

164

What's proven in PASS;
is proven on the

6. Deadly Court – The "*scales*" of generating degeneration

{Correcting violating, corrupting and abusing – Developing Scientific Trials.}

As the following diagram proves, the Deadly Court is the "*scales*" of generating degeneration.

"Injustice anywhere is a threat to justice everywhere."
- *Martin Luther King, Jr.*

The Law Doctor

What's gamed in court;
is forced onto the streets.
streets.

166

What's proven in PASS;
is proven on the

Standing on the edge of a lake of fire is like using the current Deadly Court.

Details regarding the design of Leverage Court Static Dynamics:

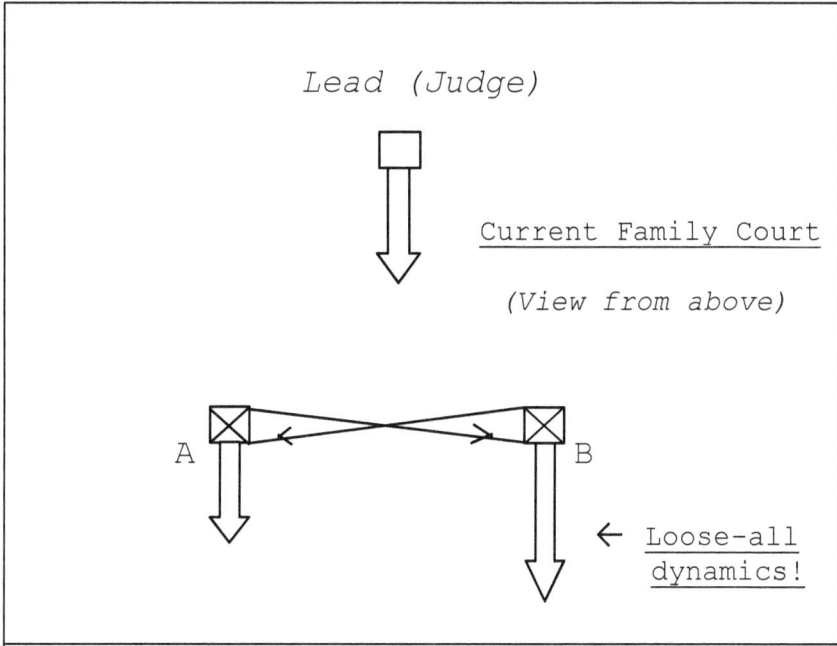

Lead (Judge)

Current Family Court

(View from above)

A   B

← Loose-all
dynamics!

The Deadly Court is a virtually loose-all design where the *"winner"* is the side that can most degenerate the other side.

Though it can only be unstable, the leadership of this system is the most intense catalyst and the greatest force on earth. It is officially approved,

What's gamed in court; is forced onto the streets.

What's proven in PASS; is proven on the streets.

officer enforced and professionally encouraged.

Practice A and practice B in the above diagram is to cause the utmost painful leverage to divide their two people in permanent and perpetual opposition. Even if it means dividing their respective professionals.

This life altering static dynamic effects humanity, morality, civility, professions and reality all at the same.

Helpless people are compelled by the threat of force and/or "law" (pressures of Leverage) to follow the lead of this three times negated, self-fulfilling implications. Implications which tend victims only towards not only psychological disorders, but towards physical disorders as well.

Both sides are demoted, suppressed and/or traumatized regardless.

Which naturally oppresses the children who, like adults, learn to follow implications that are greater than their own vocabulary. They can't even describe their pain and suffering. Or the cause. It's virtually unspeakable. They simply have to accept all of the bad effects.

There are no incentives to improve this system for the people. Only financial and vanity incentives to "im-

prove" the system for its practice of worsening society.

"Throughout history, it has been the inaction of those who could have acted; the indifference of those who should know better; the silence of the voice of justice when it mattered most; that has made it possible for evil to triumph."
- *Haile Selassie*

The Deadly Court naturally divides and conquers everything and everyone. It's permanently and perpetually inhumane. It's permanently and perpetually insane. And it's permanently and perpetually unjust.

{All Rights, Responsibilities & Interpretations Reserved for Upright USA.]

"Abide in me, and I in you. As the branch cannot bear fruit of its self, unless it abides in the vine, neither can you, unless you abide in Me.

"I am the vine, you are the branches. He who abides in Me, and I in him, bears much fruit; for without Me you can do nothing.

"If anyone does not abide in Me, he is cast out as a branch and is withered; and they gather them and throw them into the fire, and they are burned.

"If you abide in Me, and My words abide in you, you will ask what you desire, and it shall be done for you.

"By this My Father (LOVE) is glorified, that you bear much fruit; so you will be My disciples.

"As the Father loved Me, I also have loved you; abide in My love.

"If you keep My commandments, you will abide in My love, just as I have kept My Father's commandments and abide in His love.

"These things I have spoken to you, that My joy may remain in you, and that your joy may be full.

"This is My commandment, that you love one another as I have loved you.

"Greater love has no one than this, than to lay down one's life for his friends. - Jesus Christ

Our Forefathers also laid down their lives for their friends. And our Forefathers had a dream. But this today is not it.

So today more than ever we must love our enemies.

Tough love and/or tender love is on them. At least they have an option.

"My food is to do the will of Him who sent Me, and to finish His work."

"Do you not say, 'There are still four months and then comes the harvest?' Behold, I say to you, lift up your eyes and look at the fields, for they are already white for harvest!"

"And he who reaps receives wages, and gathers fruit for eternal life, that both he who sows and he who reaps may rejoice together."

"For in this saying is true: 'One sows and another reaps.'"

"I sent you to reap that for which you have not labored, and you have entered into their labors."

- Jesus Christ

The Law Doctor

What's gamed in court;
is forced onto the streets.
streets.

172

What's proven in PASS;
is proven on the

Those "*Scales*" of Generating Degeneration

Those "*scales*" of generating degeneration are obviously from the Devil himself. Because they sow and reap from exactly the opposite of what we are told.

Why is the self-posturing, crafty Weegie Wedging needed to uphold silver scales? Because only they are detached from reality.

Of course silver scales have silver tongues.
Of course having silver tongues mean a silver congress.
Of course a silver congress means a silver world.
Of course a silver world means victimized victimized victimized victims forever.
Of course bullies are ordered to figuratively "*bully*" and literally Bully inferiors.

What do you think this is? The uniting states of America?
No, it's the dividing state Bar's.

What's gamed in court;
is forced onto the streets.
streets.

173

What's proven in PASS;
is proven on the

Degeneration is the process of degenerating.

This is common and now a compulsive pattern from all of the inherently Deadly Courts.

For example, when the Supreme Court decided that providing contraceptives were to be enforced legally as part of the national "*Healthcare*" Act, but then legally excluded them from being enforced in the Hobby Lobby® case, then who should be liable?

Who should pay for their own mistakes?

But who does pay for their mistakes and suffer from the consequences of their mistakes?

These "*scales*" (generating degeneration) obviously benefits its exclusively deceptive practice at the expense, pain and suffering of lives.

And we all know that impossible silver scales must have impossible silver tongues just to stay in business.

And then impossible silver policies to protect their impossible jobs at the expense of humanity.

They have the sources to ignite and stay warm by their own burning fires consuming the rest of us on the side.

But we don't even have any means of putting out those fires.

The Law Doctor

While they're free to start them
where ever and whenever. And to fan the
flames.

Silly little silver foes. Why do you
even have a growing nose?

Is this why you won't let us know?
Or is it because you don't even know?

Oh come on now, just let us go.

At least let us switch on the
lights?

Light always equals a better show.

What's gamed in court;
is forced onto the streets.
175
What's proven in PASS;
is proven on the
streets.

The Law Doctor

What's gamed in court;
is forced onto the streets.
streets.

176

What's proven in PASS;
is proven on the

<u>Please join me in Operation "Flip Vics Switch."</u> An Operation dedicated to higher standards. Meant to flip out of pocket victims of error back into the light of truth, honor and respect.

And on into being members of the life again with healing solutions.

"Human progress is neither automatic nor inevitable.... Every step toward the goal of justice requires sacrifice, suffering, and struggle; the tireless exertions and passionate concern of dedicated individuals."

- *Martin Luther King, Jr.*

The Law Doctor

What's gamed in court;
is forced onto the streets.
streets.

178

What's proven in PASS;
is proven on the

HEALING SOLUTIONS

What's gamed in court;
is forced onto the streets.
streets.

179

What's proven in PASS;
is proven on the

The Law Doctor

What's gamed in court;
is forced onto the streets.
streets.

180

What's proven in PASS;
is proven on the

7. The Lively PASS

{Discovering life - Human Order.}

Happiness is found in surviving the impossible old, discovering the possible anew, and then sharing both with all of those who are still but a few.

"All successful people men and women are big dreamers. They imagine what their future could be, ideal in every respect, and then they work every day toward their distant vision, that goal or purpose."
- *Brian Tracy*

The Law Doctor

What's gamed in court;
is forced onto the streets.
streets.

182

What's proven in PASS;
is proven on the

The Lively PASS System

This Family Friendly, Lively PASS is ideal.

Details regarding the design of the author's Family Friendly, Lively "*Court*" PASS Static Dynamics:

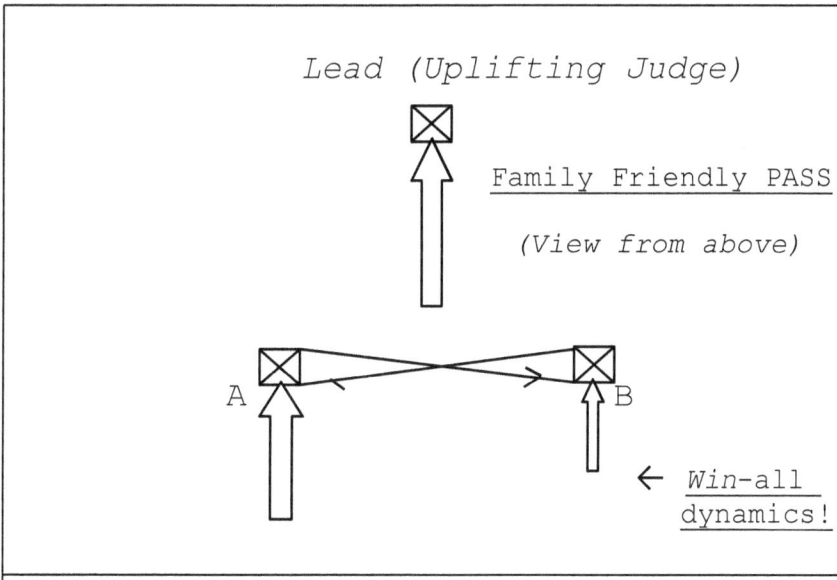

Lead (Uplifting Judge)

Family Friendly PASS

(View from above)

A   B

← Win-all dynamics!

The Lively PASS is a win-all design where everyone benefits.

"*The*" winner is the side that best promotes the other side. It's an ideal family venue since both sides, and inherently their offspring, are optimized, promoted and encouraged.

Children are the rightful benefactors being naturally and most powerfully optimized by their own parents and the highest leading implications alike just like a human incubator. Implications beyond our own vocabulary.

And the benefits would work themselves into all aspects of society, our economy, governments and the world.

Legal optimism like legal pessimism with the most powerful and catalytic force has to be the most contagious. Which is also the Law of Leverage Order. (As opposed to the Law of Leverage Disorder.)

The Deadly Court plus the Lively PASS together would be competitively complimentary. They can and should co-exist. One should handle material things. While the other should handle human issues.

The Lively PASS naturally unites and builds. It's permanently and perpetually humane. It's permanently and perpetually sane. And it's permanently and perpetually just.

{All Rights, Responsibilities & Interpretations Reserved for Upright USA.}

8. The healthy Court-PASS

{Higher Standards, Healing Humanity
and/or Incubating Truth.}

This Humane and Healthy Court-PASS
is a combination of the Deadly Court and
Lively PASS.

"For the eyes of the LORD run to and
fro throughout the whole earth, to show
Himself strong on behalf of those whose
heart is loyal to Him."

The Law Doctor

The Healthy Court-PASS System

Details regarding the design of the author's Healthy Court-PASS Static Dynamics:

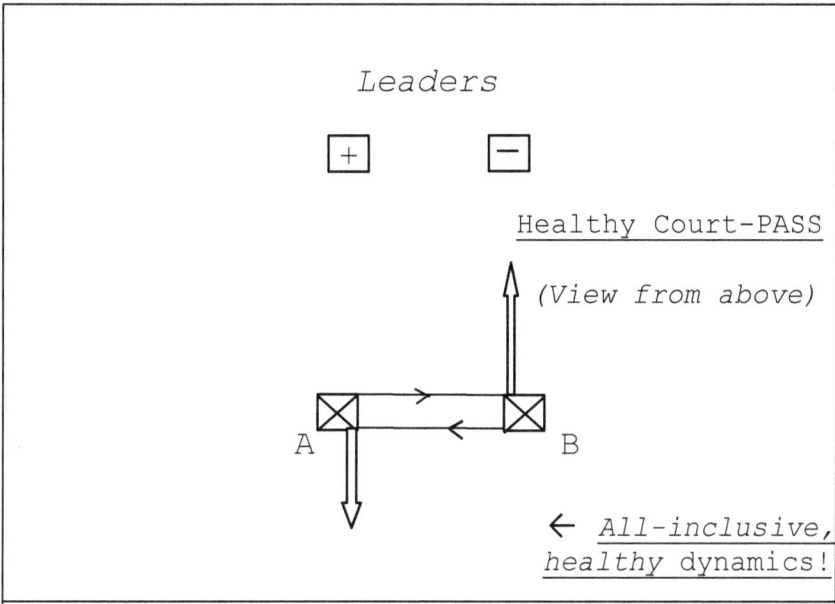

Leaders

Healthy Court-PASS

(View from above)

A   B

← *All-inclusive, healthy* dynamics!

The Humane and Healthy Court-PASS should have one vested optimist leader and one vested pessimist leader.

Each leader would score each litigant from their relative perspectives, encourage notes, and a Constitutional jury would authorize Rule, rules and rulers.

Being that some people are optimists by nature and others are pessimists by nature, this Court-PASS was born out of necessity. Because the two don't relate. They only instinctively deviate.

The Healthy Court-PASS is also competitively complimentary in of itself. It's ideally healthy.

The Healthiness results from the positive plus negative nucleus that any healthy organism absolutely needs just to survive.

And this healthy nucleus spreads throughout the entire county, country and world.

It's a no-loose, or win-all design. The common strategy of the Upright USA Race and Family Matters Mission.

The Healthy Court-PASS naturally enlightens. It's permanently and perpetually healthy. It's permanently and perpetually just. And it's permanently and perpetually contagious.

What's gamed in court; is forced onto the streets.

What's proven in PASS; is proven on the streets.

9. The Revelation Center

{This is the only possible way to truly
learn and improve all aspects of life,
society, economy and country!}

What's gamed in court;
is forced onto the streets.
streets.

189

What's proven in PASS;
is proven on the

The Law Doctor

What's gamed in court;
is forced onto the streets.
streets.

190

What's proven in PASS;
is proven on the

Scientific Trials
& Spot Trials Live!
- - - - - - - - - -

THE REVELATION
CENTER

"Sharing Burdens, discovering life
and/or realizing cures."

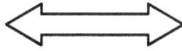

What's gamed in court;
is forced onto the streets.
streets.

191

What's proven in PASS;
is proven on the

O   Because inner-face is better than face-to-face or replace-a-face.
O   Above **all**, people need a legitimate voice!
O   Above **all**, people should be legitimately heard!
O   A Democratic jury would authorize any & all parties.
O   There would be no need for "*all authority, but no responsibility,*" uncorrectable quagmires.
O   Researchers learn, document, publish, and then polish.
O   Avoids taxing trickery and its dire consequences.
O   The Scientific Trials are Constitutional times infinity.
O   There is no chance for taxation without representation.

Scientific Trials and Spot Trials Live are not even possible in hiding Leverage Court.

And discovering plus writing plus publishing plus jury plus wise counsel plus inclusive participation under no false pretenses plus promotion equals the ultimate in accountability.

Better Trials 4 better life 4 better law
4 better people 4 better world.

Scientific Trials equal Humane
Principles times Sane Order times
Scientific Standards times Scientific
Psychology times Engineered Governments
all by and for the same. Attributes not
even legal in old courts.

The Law of Static Dynamic Leverage
Order causes not only healthy psychological effects, but also healthy
psychological attraction. All with
inherent financial benefits just the
same.

Scientific Trials and Spot Trials
Live naturally discovers. And then
applies those discoveries into
appropriate actions. And naturally
spreads.

{All Rights, Responsibilities & Interpretations
Reserved for The Founding Fathers of the United
States of America. Yes, this was their design!}

What's gamed in court;
is forced onto the streets.   193   *What's proven in PASS;*
streets.   *is proven on the*

The Law Doctor

What's gamed in court;
is forced onto the streets.
streets.

What's proven in PASS;
is proven on the

10. Discovering PBBA (Parent Blocking Bullyism Abuse)

{Tricked out kidnapping or trickled away Rights?}

How can a grandfather live with himself physically stepping between a father & his son after a baseball game and herding the son out the other way?

How can a grandfather live with himself stepping between a father & his son in life and herding the son the other way?

How do we live with ourselves stepping between our Heavenly Father & His Son and herding people the other way?

Now, I'm not much better than my child's parent-blocker, but when one's 6'4" and the others 5'7" (on the good leg) & 5'5" (on the bad leg) then the Laws of Physics come into play.

What's a father to do when court's the automatic masters of "*Rights*" being tricked-out, and official "*Responsibilities*" being tricked away? Of herding children, humanity and sanity far, far the other way?

"Most assuredly, I say to you, he who does not enter the sheepfold by the door, but climbs up some other way, the same is a thief and a robber.

"But he who enters by the door is the shepherd of the sheep..

"To him the doorkeeper opens, and the sheep hear his voice...

"Most assuredly, I say to you, I am the door of the sheep.

- *Jesus*

What's gamed in court;
is forced onto the streets.
streets.

196

What's proven in PASS;
is proven on the

The Cure to Thieves & Robbers:

Well, when the system is over 6'
times millions and the other is just me
then the Laws of *I R Physics* come into
play;
 This Law of the Lord proves that one
plus Him equals infinity;
 You see Bullyism times *"bullyism"*
robs every one of our dignity;
 Thieves are a needless waste of
time, money, physics, momentum &
emotions, not to mention health and
sanity;
 How much saner would mom, dad &
children be if bullies exponentially
times *"bullies"* would just let us be?

 Scientific Standards, now there's
our way out;
 It's far from the other limb, but it
even enlightens some of them without a
doubt;
 So there's where the Lord and I will
finally make our stand.

 Human Authority, now there's our way
to defend;
 It's far from the old branch, but it
even protects some of them.

What's gamed in court;
is forced onto the streets.   197   *What's proven in PASS;*
is proven on the
streets.

The Law Doctor

They call them sane principles, now
there's a novel idea;
It's far from the old poisonous
leaves, but it even cures some of them.

What's gamed in court;
is forced onto the streets.
streets.

198

What's proven in PASS;
is proven on the

PBBA

PBBA is Parent Blocking Bullyism Abuse.

Judicial PBBA is the most severe form of absolute physical Bullyism infinitely times intellectual "*bullyism*" (trickery) now known to mankind.

PBBA causes permanent & perpetual suppression, traumatization & even potentially fatal side effects.

PBBA is especially bad on its most helplessly dependent victims, and on its most helplessly dependent institutions.

Like tricksters who can & will mislead both dad & son just so that they'll never meet, "*bullyism*" is easy when there are no boundaries.

In fact, it was impossible to defend against since the same "*boundaries*" (NONE) are what's practiced and upheld in court.

Given that it has been Scientifically established that Courts enforce that it is illegal not to PBBA victimized victims, and that county departments of Mental Health are now known to be liable in full compliance with PBBA, the Discoverer & founder of anew has claimed any & all rights, responsibilities & interpretations to

What's gamed in court;
is forced onto the streets.   199   *What's proven in PASS;*
streets.   *is proven on the*

Human Authority with Scientific Standards to incubate truth and True Law Anew.

In effect, Scientific Justice & Scientific Psychiatry. Now *"competing"* with Psychotic *"Justice"* & Sociopathic *"Psychiatry."*

Because I for one don't even believe that intimidating bullies and *"bullies"* realize how dangerous they really are.

But I've felt PBBA's victimization's 280 times now so far.

After all, it's well known that those carrying force can & will formally brainwash their own *"criminals"* (victims) if and when accused, or even assume to be accused, of wrong doing.

And all it takes is for the victims (or patients in psychiatrists cases) to believe it. Or if they simply give into the bullies and/or *"bullies"* pressure even if they don't believe it and let it go just to get over their discomfort under duress.

And after all, isn't it a crime not to?

And if a sociopathic psychiatrist is involved, isn't it against doctors' orders not to believe them?

People who mischarge and misdiagnose others for selfish gain have a free will choice whether to do it or not. They do not have to victimize their own victims.

What's gamed in court;
is forced onto the streets.   200   *What's proven in PASS;*
is proven on the
streets.

But their victims on the other hand have no choice but to accept it and/or die trying to fight it up hill all the while looking like the bad (or sick) guy.

I, like so many others, was forced into this fight.

I'm now forced to fight just to stay alive.

In the end, one has ultimate responsibility. One does not.

The one's violating responsibility can keep forcing "*responsibility*" onto their own victims.

But I was forced to have no choice just to stay alive.

But now I'm in full compliance with the sameness of defiance. (Only without the force and trickery parts.)

And I'm in better than full compliance with their decaying defiance.

And that's the difference between scientific standards and judge "*mental*" standards. One is always right. And the other is always wrong. REGARDLESS!

The Law Doctor

What's gamed in court;
is forced onto the streets.
streets.

202

What's proven in PASS;
is proven on the

INCUBATING CURES

What's gamed in court;
is forced onto the streets.
streets.

203

What's proven in PASS;
is proven on the

The Law Doctor

What's gamed in court;
is forced onto the streets.
streets.

204

What's proven in PASS;
is proven on the

11. The Humanitarian PASS Proposal

{An urgent Petition for help with an independent Race and an intervention Mission.}

This is an urgent petition on humanitarian grounds to invite all to join our independent Race and intervention Mission.

And to invite Congress to help us and not the machine so much.

A Race and Mission to fulfill the need of higher standards, healing solutions, developing truth, incubating truth and reasoning towards under-standing within the labels of Upright USA, Family Matters Mission, {PASS}[2] and Resolve, respectfully. This is *I R Physics* realized. A gift from God. A universal "*experiment*" (Law.)

A humanitarian judicial system would

be subject to the Lord, the United States Constitution, Scientific Trials, Scientific Psychology, and Scientific Laws for Engineered Governments with Family respect and intellectual respect.

A humanitarian judicial system is needed as all evidence and proof confirms that We the People are suffering from an irreparable psychological genocide from the old system without any legitimate method, motive or means to even questioning it.

People have the Right to humane treatment. People have the need for sane treatment.

By a small mountain of evidence on file, and actions made public, their enforced, exploited, unprotected and neglected Abusive Power Disorder (APD) appears to be the norm.

While permanent and perpetual expense, pain and suffering is typical and encouraged.

In fact, wasted expense, needless pain and instinctive sufferings actually enables the old system regardless.

All the while people and the People's Rights, voice and will carry little, no, and/or negative weight.

The old system has been conformed over time and job security needs to fit the vial of ruling posterity, not the

People.

Yet the most basic need for human survival without an overload of oppression still exists. Basic needs currently unable to be accounted for.

In fact, I do believe that that is the permanent, unshakeable grounds for the United States of America.

This petition will be the most humble means at seeking justice not only publicly, but with the help of other ruling Democratic bodies as well.

An Act or act(s) supporting an independent, humanitarian judicial system(s) on humanitarian grounds.

Grounds that do not currently exist.

Grounds that have no real venue.

Grounds that are currently obstructed and/or exploited as much and as often as possible for lesser good.

Warranted grounds for a much needed, independent Upright USA Race and Family Matters Mission.

"Where there is no vision, the people perish."
—   Proverbs 29:18

What's gamed in court;
is forced onto the streets.

207

What's proven in PASS;
is proven on the
streets.

The Law Doctor

What's gamed in court;
is forced onto the streets.
streets.

What's proven in PASS;
is proven on the

12. A new asylum from old system amnesty

Upright USA with Family Matters

    The Law Doctor of America respect-
fully requests permission from the People
to establish a new Race and a new Mission
to both prevent automatic victimizations
and to protect victims of the old due to
current threat levels that are often
intolerable and progressively deviating
worse and that have no known avenue for
remediation.
    And because a few of us have no
capacity for negligence.

    "Change your thoughts and change
your world."
    - Norman Vincent Peale

What's gamed in court;
is forced onto the streets.   209   *What's proven in PASS;*
is proven on the
streets.

Pioneering the way to separation today must be a must to uphold not only the authority of the United States Constitution, but the authority of humanity and of sanity alike.

It has proven to be punished as a permanent, perpetual, ongoing crime to live under Constitutional Rights and Humane Order. (Even though that's the only way possible.)

While the old exclusively licensed practice, with their own "*seal*" of authority being upheld, and the new have only divisional differences at heart.

"Believe you can and you're halfway there."
- Theodore Roosevelt

The courthouse's only acceptable practice with its own "*seal*" of approval has the only enforcement and policy capitalization.

The current practice has conspired to overthrow governments, juries, Democracies and enforcements alike by and for demoting the same within themselves.

It is well known that some of us are willing and able to promote Rights,

Humanity and Sanity to legally exist and are in dire need of a new asylum from old system amnesty.

We risk life and limb while suffering greatly to expertly experience and scientifically establish that constitutional Rights violations and humane treatment violations exist permanently and perpetually out of control and without remedy.

"Don't judge each day by the harvest you reap but by the seeds that you plant."

-Robert Louis Stevenson

No supporting Leverage, Law or Order currently exists to protect our Humanity, Rights and Sanity.

"I can't change the direction of the wind, but I can adjust my sails to always reach my destination."

- Jimmy Dean

Being a survivor of the old Death Trap, the founder of anew has the RIGHT to exist.

The founder of anew has US

constitutional discovery Rights to intellectual property gained researching and discovering the problems with the old. And to any and all solutions to such problems which may or may not yet exist.

"We can't help everyone, but everyone can help someone."
- Ronald Reagan

The old practice has a known history of compromising both physical and intellectual property.

While being detached from reality themselves the old practice that's upheld is known to defer, steal and destroy both intellectual and physical reality solely for selfish gains.

The founder's race and mission in life has proven to be to intervene with Human Authority using scientific standards and healing solutions for engineered governments, humane order and Project Peace Police appeal.

"Oh mother of a mighty race,
Yet lovely in thy youthful grace!

The elder dames, thy haughty peers,
Admire and hate thy blooming years."
   - William Cullen Bryant

It only makes counterproductive
sense for engineers, surgeons,
psychiatrists, doctors, designers and the
likes to be subject to enforced
divisional disordering dynamics.
   And it's well known that the old
judicial enterprise is one of disorder
that profits and postures with respect to
disordering.
   Which is bad, even deadly (dire I
say murderous) for any society and
economy.
   A handicap on America and the world
of Biblical proportions!

   "It is during our darkest moments
that we must focus to see light."
   - Aristotle Onassis

   "True happiness comes from joy of
deeds well done, the zest of creating
things new."
   - Antoine de Saint-Exupery

What's gamed in court;
is forced onto the streets.
streets.

213

What's proven in PASS;
is proven on the

There's is not paid Bill of Rights that we're constitutionally entitled to.

Nor is it upheld taxes for supposed State Statutes that we buy into.

Yes, only they are in default. And yes, only they can and will punish us for it.

Theirs are unpaid Bills and unmet tax obligations.

Both to benefit an exclusive, foreign, and alienating Hierarchy instead.

A disordering enterprise paradigm scheme over America. The Original Ponzi.

If a most feared bully pulpit or "*bully*" job title above a real live human being says that a person is guilty or "*guilty,*" or an "*unfit parent,*" or "*whatever*" then that is instinctively arranged with leverage as unquestionable "*law & order*" (Leverage & Disorder) [BE SUPPRESSED AND/OR DIE!] Not decided on by free will inclusively by a Democracy. But decided on against free will by the self-serving wills of exclusive profiteers.

It's intimidating fear trickled-down divisionally.

All at tax payers expense.

And all at tax payers sufferance.

But fraudulently under the sworn pretense of providing each and everyone one of us with legitimate Bill of Rights

Due Process paid in full.

While only those doing the delusioning are those who are detached from reality.

It's a Rope-a-Dope & Ride Piggyback practice. From foreign and alienating job titles to foreign and alienating mechanics.

It's an MMD that automatically Weegie Wedges.

A common law and case "*law*" deceptive practice.

We have Right to protection and healing from corrupting and inhumane abusing. Yet none exists.

What's worse is that very few have the ability and experience to work on discoveries if this magnitude.

We just might be in too deep now.

Bar associated judges and attorney's dividing practice is upheld in the old systems.

Aaron W. Wemple's uniting practice will be upheld in the new systems.

Both cannot relate, only deviate.

So to avoid contact and inherently ruining each other, separation today is a must.

And because in the old system the new is routinely punished by the old for their crimes too.

All authority with no

responsibilities was a monumental error.

Because a chain of corrupting and inhumanity commanding is no place for men, women or children.

A chain of corrupting and inhumanity commanding instead of a Democracy can steal, kill and destroy from hidden places that few can even think to endeavor.

The pioneer's Race in life to engineer governments, and mission to heal humanity ought to be reason enough to accept a new asylum from old system amnesty.

However, other discoveries have already developed.

Including work on non-lethal and non-illegal vehicles, systems of the light, new *I R physics*, certified Americans, licensed authors, sanctified speakers, etc.

These are but a few of the rewards to come.

And because licensing underneath of a foreign and alienating Authority and "*authority*" is treason anyway. Treason of the highest ORDER.

The Law Doctor

"I have always considered it as treason against the great republic of human nature, to make any man's virtues the means of deceiving him."
- Samuel Johnson

"Disunion by force is treason."
- Andrew Jackson

Being "*bad*" and Bad is figuratively and literally the lowest level and "*Highest*" system of treason.

What's gamed in court;
is forced onto the streets.
streets.

217

What's proven in PASS;
is proven on the

The Law Doctor

What's gamed in court;
is forced onto the streets.
streets.

218

What's proven in PASS;
is proven on the

13. Who wants True Democracy?

Why not consider Law & Leverage equally?
Why not consider People & Parties equally?

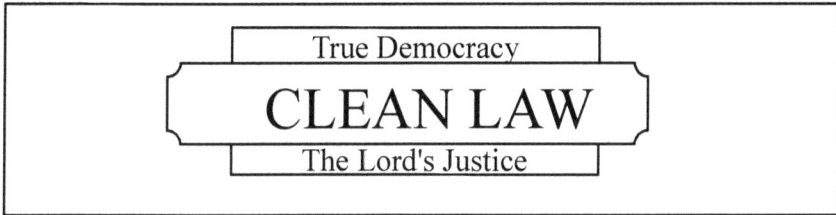

True Democracy
CLEAN LAW
The Lord's Justice

Why not consider brains & brawn equally?
Why not democracy & dictators equally?
Why not consider life & death equally?

Clean Law is now
designing systems upright.
(After dyeing from systems down-low.)

What's gamed in court;
is forced onto the streets.
streets.

219

What's proven in PASS;
is proven on the

Why let intellectual thumb knots have all the fun authorizing final rule?
Especially since their 21st Century crucifixion is impossible compliance that's illegal to defy?!
Why not consider legitimate standards along with illegitimate standards equally in the university & therefore beyond?
Why not consider scientific standards & contrasting, contrary and/or trickery standards in the courtroom & therefore below?
Why not consider Truthhood and Falsehood equally?
Why not Sane Principles & Insane Principles alike?
Why not Human Authority & Deaths Authority?
Why not consider Heaven & Hell equally?

Why not consider right & wrong equally?
Why not honesty & deception equally?
Why not unite & divide equally?
Why not truth & error equally?
Why not {PASS}² & Court?
Why not True Autonomous Democracy?

July 4, 2014

Dearly beloved:

Thank you so much for your help with the cold case and hot cause. I know that this is difficult.

With your support our communities will prosper and its leadership will improve dramatically. All the while truly protecting and serving our most vulnerable children and our most valuable institutions.

I'd like to take this opportunity to properly introduce to you The Upright USA Race & Family Matters Mission. Both with higher standards and healing solutions. Both that inherently develop incubating truth.

Engineering systems upright is all that we can possibly do.

Because growing towards light is the essence of life.

And growing towards life is the essence of light.

Please consider the Truth, Good & Bad, in Education and then beyond.

Please consider the Truth, Good & Bad, in Justice and then below.

And please consider the Truth in

What's gamed in court;
is forced onto the streets.
streets.

221

What's proven in PASS;
is proven on the

Education Bill(s), True Democracy & the Truth in Justice Acts all by & for Human Authority with Scientific Standards.

    And please join me in the 21st Century! Because neglect of this magnitude is far worse than a crime today. And because cutting corners at other people's expense financially, physically & psychologically was so B.C.

        With Jesus blood in my veins,
        Aaron W. Wemple

Why Dictatorships ruling over Democracies may not have been such a good idea after all:

Aaron W. Wemple, father of victimized children, husband of victimized wife, and perpetually victimized victim himself begged the accused Bar associates for years not to Neglect their own practices. Yet they did.

But all Bar associated judges and attorneys swore under oath a verbal contract publicly with the People to remain subject to the United States Constitution.

While the People implied agreement.

The United States Constitution clearly ORDERS that "**all**" cases (people) equal a Democratic "**jury**" (People) authority.

Yet Bar associates practice and uphold that all cases (people) equal Dictative (Bar) authority.

They and I agree to go one direction. But I get arrested, charged, imprisoned, Neglected by officials and prosecuted for it.

And then I have to pay one of them money and loyalty just to get any help with their violating me.

Financially, it pays them infinitely well to mislead (violate) as often as

What's gamed in court; is forced onto the streets. 223 *What's proven in PASS; is proven on the streets.*

possible.

Politically, it benefits with infinite subjecthood to mislead (violate) as often as possible.

When you're the finalizing group then leading by misleading is infinitely lucrative.

And you're the finalizing group then leading by misleading is infinitely subjectable.

From the groups perspective, it's infinitely leverageable, infinitely excusive and therefore inherently infinitely abusive.

From the People's perspective, it's infinitely expensive, infinitely suppressing and infinitely traumatizing. It's like a never ending, needlessly expensive, needlessly painful bug zapper that's illegal not to touch.

Dictative "*order*" (schemes and regimes) are scientifically known to be impossible except to tax plus suppress and/or traumatize.

"*Spinning*" victims (a common, well-known judicial tactic in America) under duress is suppression victimization.

And **SHRINKING** victims (a well-known judicial operation in America) under duress is traumatic victimization.

But "*spinning*" and **SHRINKING** children under duress with authority (a

What's gamed in court;
is forced onto the streets.   224   *What's proven in PASS;*
streets.   *is proven on the*

well-known operation) who are not only naive, but helplessly dependent on it is programing a fatal alarm clock to go off stabbing themselves in the back repeatedly over and over again if and whenever they eventually realize what happened, who got hurt, whose fault it was, and why they were tricked into living their whole life suppressed and/or traumatized.

And they routinely without conscious victimize me and my children simply because we are their victims. In fact, they actually believe that they are following the law by doing it!

Dictators ruling over Democracies was not such a good idea after all. It absolutely causes mental illnesses, abuses and child abuses. Instinctively!

The Law Doctor

What's gamed in court;
is forced onto the streets.
streets.

What's proven in PASS;
is proven on the

What's gamed in court;
is forced onto the streets.
streets.

227

What's proven in PASS;
is proven on the

The Law Doctor

What's gamed in court;
is forced onto the streets.
streets.

What's proven in PASS;
is proven on the

14. Overcoming fool's gold

Silver Universities
teach
silver scales
make
silver tongues
need
silver congress
forces
divided people
enforces
against honorable intentions
and
finally upholds only illegitimate
activities.

What's gamed in court;
is forced onto the streets.
streets.

229

What's proven in PASS;
is proven on the

The Law Doctor

What's gamed in court;
is forced onto the streets.
streets.

230

What's proven in PASS;
is proven on the

How targeted terrorism against constitutional Christian parents & helplessly dependent children has overthrown governments

It has been firmly established, scientifically proven and legitimately experienced that all unamended Bill of RIGHTS that are not upheld are an abusive, enforced form of premeditated terrorism.

A targeted terrorism by the controlling associates knowingly against constitutional Christian parents, helplessly dependent children, and our most valuable institutions.

Constitutional Christian's and the likes are known to be indoctrinated and fully vested in following the truth. As are children's natural tendencies. So we are the easy targets for misleaders to use and abuse. Because constitutional Christian parents and the likes would naturally follow constitution truths. Especially since the controlling associate's swore under oath that they would stay in line with the United States constitution too. And not selfish and misleading *"interpretation"* operations hiding way out in left field somewhere.

So naturally, healthy, obvious and mutually agreed upon Bill of Rights from

the United States Constitution would be
expected to be paid in full.   If not,
truth followers can't be expected to go
there. And who would even suspect
anything otherwise except misleaders?

Fathers are known to protect their
families and the guidance of governing
forces against unhealthy distractions,
deadly obstacles and neglectfully
disordering.

And it's now known that the road
ahead for our most precious children and
our most valuable institutions are
enforced to be disordered.

So, any good father who has taught
his children to obey the truth must
either straighten the road out ahead, or
else sit back and watch his children bump
through life to become more and more
disordered forever.

A masterhood of falsehood now
authorizes any excuse that they choose
just to secure their own glory based
solely on disorder. An automatic targeted
terrorism only against constitutional
Christian parents in the ruse of government authority was the Devil's master
plan now perfected. His children simply
follow his lead.

Unconstitutionally dictating
falsely, or judging by 3rd-hand account
between the "*best*" sin or sin, or "*best*"

2nd-hand false witnesses is building the enemies empire while stabbing constitutional Christian parents right in the face.

Except the occasional obvious murder or rape proper sentence, there is no possible way to do any lasting good or to have any lasting value from a deadly system like this. It's purely evil by and for evil's sake.

The old system is intentionally counterintuitive to constitutional Christian parents for a reason.

"*Justice*" is obviously not for all today. "*Justice*" is more for the Devil first, and for the exclusive disordering entrepreneurs second. It builds evil and destroys good.

And this type of now unquestionable, absolute power abuse is why the United States of America came to be. It's exactly what our United States Constitution is all about protecting people from.

And it's this absolute, unequally unquestionable authority abuse against constitutional Christian parents that is ruining America and our children today.

And when salt loses its flavor it's good for nothing.

Parasites only consume what life produces. Life producers consume and

What's gamed in court;
is forced onto the streets.
streets.

233

What's proven in PASS;
is proven on the

produce. But good life producers produce more than they consume.

Parasites don't care. They just take.

Parasitic practices are unconscious by the nature of things and have no choice but to exploit and consume the results of producer's works.

However, this is not logic, healthy or sane for social, family or economic order. In fact, it's illogical, unhealthy and insane social, family and economic disordering.

Those who become accustom to exploiting the producers of real things of real value eventually become spoiled and irrational.

And when the producers have been completely exhausted of everything, then the unconscious parasitic practice has no conscious choice but to try and try to pressure or trick the producers to give them something because they've gone too far and cannot comprehend that the producer just can't produce anymore. This has been established. This is historical. And this is academic.

It's like terrorizing babies for silence. If a baby cries they assume that if they beat the baby then they'll make it stop crying. And at some point there is no turning back. And at some point, especially when it pays them well and is seen as illegal to stop, then beating the baby under the ruse of chasing the biggest ghost that they can dream up until it dies is just business as usual.

In the end they'll say, "Wow...we really did murder America."

So, if you're a constitutional Christian parent, they don't even realize it, but their targeted terrorism is against you and your children.
If you are a tax payer then you are supporting targeted terrorism against constitution Christian parents and their helplessly dependent children that has overthrown governments.

If you are crying like a baby, or barking like a rabid dog backed into the corner of a cage, then beware, because your end is near. Especially since blankets of oppression keep falling like presents but stick like glue and stuck sucking like ticks.

Rodney King once said, "why can't we all just get along?!"
Well Rodney, may you rest in peace, but pride of this magnitude and benefits this ease are just way too strong and

just way too out of control. People must die at the hands of their abusers before shared consciousness even starts to wake up.

It's just way too tightening of vice and vise devices down here in the Devil's trap. There's just no turning back.

But maybe ditching the mold and starting over anew?

Instead of protecting humanity, current officers and officials may feel compelled (if by nothing else routine) to protect the targeted terrorists beating babies and pushing dogs instead of baby lovin', dog pettin', constitutional Christian parents. Our True Americans.

15. Severing schools sever courts sever worlds

After reading a Playboy article (June 2014 edition) entitled "TREATMENT COMPLEX – Can effective mental health treatment exist in a criminal justice system driven by profit?" I legitimately understand.

No disrespect, but the bigger question is – Can effective mental health treatment exist under court associates rule being politically and price fixed?

Far too often mental health "*treatment*" is simply leverage to help submit a victim before trial and/or weaken a victim's case for trial.

All of us who have courtroom exper-ience know that we can be "*spun*" and/or **SHRUNK** by and for the exclusively li-censed disorder entrepreneur's running our courts.

What's gamed in court;
is forced onto the streets.   237   *What's proven in PASS;*
is proven on the streets.

Though scientifically, theirs is an impossible system with impossible systematic dynamics. But, chasing their tails our helplessly dependent people's expense, it's their game, their rules and their world today.

After studying the system for almost 40 years and documenting its effects, it turns out that psychiatric counselors under the orchestration of court counselors can and will irreversibly abuse victims unspeakably with their combined powers. Probably even unknowingly. But it is suppression. Often times with the "*best*" of intentions put in mind.

But the dire effects are still the same.

While judges (who are also exclusively licensed court counselors) not only wittingly allow this, but Order it enforced to happen.

For Example, after collecting and documenting evidence against one particular court for years because they were commonly known for not only being corrupt, but for forcing other people & professions to be corrupt as well, it turns out that there are hidden Leverage rules at work. Or, hiding "*law*" (really Leverage), if you will, at work.

My competitor being in the

What's gamed in court;
is forced onto the streets.   238   *What's proven in PASS;*
is proven on the streets.

psychiatric field herself followed the
"*law*" (Leverage) scandal forced to game
the system the same way that it games us.

I was indoctrinated as a scientist
type. So I could not "*understand*"
(Leverage) this game.

The extent of severed courts
rendering severed minds is just now
starting to come to light, but it may
never be fully realized. As it has gone
on for years undetected. But much of this
abuse is intolerable to its victims. I
know of several deaths due to it. So who
could testify? And who would believe it?

Life, unlike severed practices &
severed system, has inherent consequences. Especially since severance is impossible to comply with but illegal to defy.

Of which, severed professions have a
free pass and a free ride when victims
are simply victimized to protect and
serve their co-operative hidden agenda.

When "*job security*" is the fuel and
the high and mighty have their preference
then the rest of us can and will be
either a cloud of smoke and/or a "*fire!*"
for trial. We're mute issues in court.

I stood up one day in court, with
indisputable proof of their corrupting
both psychiatrists and people, and tried
to place the judge under citizen's arrest

What's gamed in court;
is forced onto the streets.   239   *What's proven in PASS;*
is proven on the streets.

per Illinois State Statutes.

But officers grabbed me and put me back in my seat for following the law.

But I couldn't participate or else I'd be Accountable (an accessory to crime) per State Statutes. And Constitutionally, I don't have to implicate myself in crime. That's my undeniable 5th Amendment RIGHT.

So, since Neglect was also known to be ruled against, I simply repeated every word that the judge said.

I woke up two days later naked in a padded jail cell. My mother, who was at court with me, said that I was handcuffed and then tackled, choked and hit my head on the concrete floor two days ago. Three days later a guard finally snuck me in to make a phone call. I eventually saw a doctor and he said that I had a concussion.

In the mean time she heard the judge in open court Order the state's attorney to call mental health to have me "*shrunk*." (Suppressed and/or traumatized.)

Turns out, getting "*shrunk*" to fix the scales of "justice" is standard. After all, who's a jury going to believe, a professional with a suit & tie and a computer and a printer and formal report

What's gamed in court;
is forced onto the streets.   240   *What's proven in PASS;*
is proven on the streets.

form evidence, or a criminal in a yellow
jumpsuit with no report form evidence?
    And after all, who's detached from
reality?

16. Severed courts, severed minds

Make no mistake; courts are severed from reality, detached from the real world. They intimidate and/or enforce that subjected minds are detached from the real world as well. And that disproportioning severance is more important to them than reality.

It follows suit (with force if need be) that all of society must comply in reverence to the god of "*justice*" (hiding Leverage) dividing us just to protect & serve themselves if and when the need or want arises. Our sacrifices and sufferance's are their dictated offerings. And it is compulsive.

Hiding Leverage under the ruse of "*law*" has compulsive negative side effects to the rest of us besides just compulsively dividing us. Dire consequences that are automatic and even fatal.

What's gamed in court;
is forced onto the streets.   243   *What's proven in PASS;*
is proven on the streets.

For example, whether severed or not
court associates must sever or not.
Whether intimidating or not it must
intimidate or not. Whether detached from
reality or not it must detach from
reality or not. Whether corrupt or not it
must corrupt or not. Whether delusional
or not it must delusion or not. And
whether or not inherent Delusional
Paradox's (Contrasting, Contrary & Tricky
Standards that are impossible to comply
with but illegal to defy) are enforced
they must Hypocrisize. Hence, the Rule of
Intellectual Thumb Knots.

Severed & intimidating courts
obviously sever & intimidate minds. But
it's not just minds that are severed &
intimidated; it's severed & intimidated
hearts, severed & intimidated bodies,
severed & intimidated People, severed &
intimidated college students, severed &
intimidated children, and a perpetually
severed, perpetually intimidating & a
perpetually stigmatized world as is.

All with a needless waste of money
of course.

So, Scientific Trials (with Spot
Trials Live) & Scientific Psychology are
now taking on Psychotic "*Justice*" and
Sociopathic "*Psychiatry.*"

Like most systems & superiors, court

What's gamed in court;
is forced onto the streets.   244   *What's proven in PASS;*
is proven on the streets.

counselors & mental counselors are known to have each other's backs, not their helplessly dependent people and/or People.

Dependents of systems & superiors are often compulsively taken advantage of simply for being dependents.

And this follows perfectly in line with courts Contrasting, Contrary & Trickery Standards.

If one cannot comply with impossible to comply with guidance just "curse" them.

Dependents are compulsively taken advantage of since systematic report form evidence with a superior witness obviously trumps any & all incubated inferior-ated dependents with no evidence in courts Supersuperior Superrigged "*SUPERRIGGED*" Supersystems.

And since one side of the scale always has like-minded systematic "*freedom the press*" formal reports with a superior witness "*vs.*" inferior-ated, severed, intimidated, null, void and/or "*worse*" Free Speech victimized victim regardless. In other words, like universities, courts rigged.

So why not consider the Upright USA Race with Family Matters Mission? We demote Contrasting, Contrary & Trickery

What's gamed in court;
is forced onto the streets.   245   *What's proven in PASS;*
is proven on the streets.

Standards while promoting Scientific Standards. We demote corrupting and promote correcting. We demote harming and promote healing. We demote wasting money and promote saving money. Because one of us should obviously be the highest authorizing practice upheld, enforced & supported. And one should not.

So why not Human Authority?

THINKING ANEW

What's gamed in court;
is forced onto the streets.

What's proven in PASS;
is proven on the streets.

17. Thinking in 3-CCDD

{Transformational and/or Tranfigurational
thinking}

Fully thinking in the terms of Three
Complex Concurrent with Divisional Dimen-
sions (3-CCDD) is Transfigurational
Thinking.

Transfigurational Thinking is an
exclusive ability to think.

Transfigurational Thinking is
proprietary.

An example for developing Transfigurational Thinking is that law schools and
lawyers imply that they are illegal not
to follow.

Yet it is impossible to follow
physical leverage hidden behind
intellectual "*law*" in reality.

Ever see the cartoon character Wiley
Coyote "try" to run into a rock wall just

What's gamed in court;
is forced onto the streets.   249   *What's proven in PASS;*
is proven on the streets.

because there was a tunnel painted on it and a sign pointing "go here!"

There is no sane way to do it. It's impossible to follow hiding "law" as physical Leveraging force. You just keep making us run into new paintings on the wall! Plus, it's illegal not to!

So this quagmire figuratively tricks and then literally forces everyone and everything to be subject to lying.

Everyone has to lie just to "*excuse*" it whether they realize it or not. This forces everyone to follow the footsteps of the Spirit of deception.

This forces everyone to be subject to the devil instead of God and the Spirit of Truth.

After all, it's enforced as being illegal not to. (Follow the Devil that is.)

Transfigurational Thinking is now known to be proprietary. It's owned and operated by God Himself by and for but through Jesus Christ by and for but through His most vested servants.

3-CCDD thinking knows uniting & dividing at the same time.

For example, "*one person's perspective*" (Another Person's Perspective) [A THIRD PERSONS PERSPECTIVE] is thinking along the lines of not only three dimensions, but three concurrent complex dimensions.

"*One person*" (Other People) [AND A THIRD GROUP] relates attributes in terms of appropriate context and, more importantly, appropriate divisional aspects.

For example, "*inferiors*" (Officers & Officials) [AND ATTORNEYS & JUDGES] are all bound *psychologically* and/or **physically** within those boundaries inherently dividing them as well all by their implied differences.

{*Italic* font relates to *psychological* attributes. And **bold** font relates to **physical** attributes. For example, *psychological* **warfare**.}

{And **Bold** plus *italic* plus capital fonts reflect the inherent side effects, both physical and psychological, plus

What's gamed in court;
is forced onto the streets.   251   *What's proven in PASS;*
is proven on the streets.

PERMANENT AND PERPETUAL, that these wars
have on their helplessly dependent
COLLATERALLY DAMAGED victims.}

{And emphasis of divisional effects
adds accuracy. "*Feel*" (**Know**) [**OWN**] for
example. Emphasis marks reflect different
division standards. But in reverse ordering.}

{These concurrent dimensions instinctively grow as do their inherent
differences.}

In a relationship for example, "*love*"
(**Love**) [**AND LOVE**] obviously means three
different things with three different
affects from three different perspectives.

Likewise, three different perspectives obviously have three different
differences inherently.

The [**RULE**] of love, for example, is
outside of each and every one of us.

The (**Rule**) of love is more instinctive.

And the "*rule*" of love is all that's
subject to us.

The (**Officials**) of love are objective
and/or subjective and in the midst of us.

The "*order*" of love is subjective to
each and every one of us and/or (**Subjected**) onto us.

What's gamed in court;
is forced onto the streets. 252 *What's proven in PASS;*
is proven on the streets.

Without literally experiencing each and every feeling of love first hand it is impossible to legitimately know each and every feeling of love.

I suggest that each person's love is as unique as a snowflake. And that only they can truly own their own love snowflake.

Likewise for each person's other perspectives, interpretations & emotions.

Feelings of pride in one's own job can be just as unique. And it's obvious given the competitive nature of the human kind that pride versus pride can & will come into play.

Pride versus pride can & will have instinctive **COLLATERAL DAMAGES** worse than both damages of the two pitted against each other when on the highest stage.

Now when higher-ups "*assume*" an outside person without having first-hand experience with them then they enslave them to their own (**Assumptions)** and/or [*ASSUMPTIONS*] when they are enforced.

We limit ourselves to those "*handi-caps*" and inflict others with those **HANDICAPS.** An absolutely vulnerable place to be for everyone.

In fact, it's almost effortless to take advantage of victims from "*here*" to [*HERE*] given staged differences. It's

What's gamed in court;
is forced onto the streets.   253   *What's proven in PASS;*
is proven on the streets.

more instinctive than not.

Mix in the current liability issues that enforcements could face if they are wrong with force and it's easy to understand how one's own assumptions can trap their own victims into the same vexing vices and/or vises permanently and perpetually forever. (All through no fault of their own victims.)

After all, this is the LAW from "*law*" through (**Law**) to [**"*JUSTICE.*"**]

Just assume and go!?

Not only that, but trap their innocent victims into being forced to defend themselves from liable pride's "*assumptions*" whether their own victims know about their ulterior motive or not.

It's factually the "*law*" to the **LEVERAGED** not to know about it.

The inherent impact of "*assumptions*" on complex concurrency & divisional dimensions can & will inherently increase over time and trickery with respect to neglect. The Growing divisions actually increase with respect to negligence. The more they are neglected and/or "excused" the more they grow.

United States of America?!

Especially if the neglect is due to not even realizing it. Because it naturally seems right to those who have never

What's gamed in court;
is forced onto the streets.   254   *What's proven in PASS;*
is proven on the streets.

experienced its consequences.

But obviously, any & all "*interpre-tations*" to **INTERPRETATIONS** are irrelevant when both actions & inactions speak louder than words.

This is obvious, self-evident and can be self-proven (the only legitimate proof.)

In Christ, I myself am not subject to "*dumb*" (**Dumber)** [*AND DUMBEST CONSEQUES.*] Or else I'd be dumber than prescribing and enforcing the dumbest too.

In my Founding Fathers, I myself am not subject to "*scary*" (**Scary)** [*SCARIEST*] tactics and operations of Domestic "*Psychological*"-(**To)**-[*PHYSICAL*] Warfare JUST to generate themselves at the expense of degenerating the People "*under*" them. Or else I'd be a Wasting, Violating, Corrupting and Abusing(WVCA) Monger too.

The "*gifts*" to the innocent bystan-ders today is lack of knowledge and never really knowing. Yes, intellect is being taken from us daily by robbers and thieves.

In Christ by and through my Founding

What's gamed in court;
is forced onto the streets.   255   *What's proven in PASS;*
is proven on the streets.

Fathers I get to know before I get in-volved.

So that's where I go.

Hiding a hidden Hierarchy is subli-minal today.

Exposing it for what it truly is the dependent future of all mankind.

Otherwise, why not just eventually push a button and blow up all of those that you've "tricked" keeping them permanently and perpetually suppressed and then just spread "whatever?"

Pattern-ism is as pattern-ism does.

Citizens of America take off the "*pretty*" gloves!

What's gamed in court;
is forced onto the streets.
256
What's proven in PASS;
is proven on the streets.

18. To Hypocrisize and/or "*not*" (Leverage) to Hypocrisize?!

{Why is this our only earthly destiny?}

Silver scales must have silver tongues. Everybody knows that.

But did you know that it's illegal not to trickle down? And/or to trickle down with force?!

And that it's illegal for congress, state legislators and local governments not to abide by the silver scales and silver tongues instead of us?

The result?

COLLATERAL DAMAGES!

And I'm not just talking about simple collateral damages. I'm talking about massive collateral damages. Permanent, perpetual & eternal collateral damages.

For example, what do you do when it's

illegal not to follow a superior?

You accept it and follow along.

But what do you do when you know by experience that it's impossible to follow a superior?

You are figuratively and/or literally torn "trying" (**Impossible)** to accept it.

Thus, you're forced to follow whatever. Usually the heaviest weight and/or the most appealing attraction. But anything that is an alternative to thinking. Because "thinking" (**Impossible)** hurts too much.

As law-abiding as you are personally, then that's how hard you try to accept it.

Or, I should say, as law-abiding as you are personally, then that's how **Hard** you "try" (**Impossible)** to accept it.

So, in reality, as law-abiding as you are personally, then that's how **HARD** you are instinctively "tried" (**Impossible)** [**SUFFER!**] enforced to accept it.

Do you see the trend here?

Do you feel the pain just from the figurative sense? Do you want to try it literally?

It's impossible for those who have never experienced the full effects from the downside of this 21st Century Unconscious Crucifixion caused by

What's gamed in court;
is forced onto the streets.   258   *What's proven in PASS;*
is proven on the streets.

intellectual slip knoters to legitimately
know what it feels like.

It feels like you're suffocating
intellectually. It throbs when you are
under duress of law to even think about
it. You eventually pray that the dyeing
gets physical.

One may "*wish*" but never fix
irreparable damages.

And it's impossible for those who
have legitimately experienced this to
have an equal voice as any of those who
help cause it. So that's like a double
slip knot vice and/or vise. With double
the choking hazard intellectually and
physically.

But this is what I call being Hypocrisized. **HYPOCRISIZED** simply for
"*trying*" (**Impossible**) [*SUFFER!*] to follow
the law. Or, "*law*" (**Leverage**)
[*SUPPRESSION* AND/OR ***TRAUMATIZATION***] I
should legitimately say! Because that's
the trend.

If it hurts, then what? Hurt some
more? Yes and yes forever!

But enforcing that citizens beat
themselves up is not good policy or

What's gamed in court;
is forced onto the streets.   259   *What's proven in PASS;*
is proven on the streets.

practice. Witnesses would testify, and evidence confirms that practices know this. Policies obviously can't.

Hypocrisy Philosophies ruling over the People prescribes needlessly wasteful financial, psychological and/or physical pain and suffering permanently and per-petually forever.

Beating yourself up because detached supersuperiors prescribe it and make superiors enforce it is uncivilizing.

It is impossible for inferiors to follow but also illegal not to follow. Which is torturous.

Their *"glory"* is a Suicide Sentence **CRAVING** an ending for the rest of us who know it and feel it. Forcing alternatives to thinking because it hurts to think.

If you have never experienced these Hypocrisy Systems & Hypocrisy Superiors under the threat of eminent force then you're in for a real *"treat."* It defies your own law-abidingness to even try to understand it ahead of time.

Superiors are even generally banned by supersuperiors from experiencing this Crucifixion fully. Supersuperiors in court almost always have their back. Which makes *"law"* (**Leverage)** sense. Especially since supersuperiors from court make up the *"front."*

What's gamed in court;
is forced onto the streets.   260   *What's proven in PASS;*
is proven on the streets.

What do you do when you find out from experience, experience that neither your superior or supersuperior has, that systems you're all dependent on are illegal to defy and impossible to comply with? Let supersuperiors *"work"* it out in court!? **IMPOSSIBLE** in life!?

This is when you become **SUPER-HYPOCRISIZED**.

Being **SUPERHYPOCRISIZED** only pro-ceeds becoming Systematically Euthanized. Which your own children can and will be Systematically kidnapped for through no fault of your own. And everybody will agree with them and not with you. You're crazy and rightfully own a death wish by this time.

What do you do when it's unspeakable because it appears illegal for anyone else not to believe them instead of you? Do you:

A – **SUFFER** in silence?

B – *"Fight"* an impossible & illegal fight?

C – Get Brain tied-up and spiral into oblivion? Or

D – Stop all the insanity and start all over again?

What chance or choice did I have when it violates State Statutes, Corruption,

What's gamed in court;
is forced onto the streets.   261   *What's proven in PASS;*
is proven on the streets.

Humanity and Sanity to be Accountable
with an obvious, self-evident and self-
provable Conspiracy against (US Constitutional) Civil Rights by Supersuperiors
and Supersystems? And when it's an
obvious violation of all of the above to
Neglect them?

I'm giving back. I'm trying to
protect others from being Hypocrisized or
worse after being Superhypocrisized
myself, and nearly Systematically
Euthanized.

It's no small job today. In fact, it
has to be a revolutionary job. That's how
far gone they are.

After all, the future of all mankind
depends on it. And isn't that the debt
that I owe to others?

Heroes die for their friends.

So I'm going out with my boots **ON!**

"*Forget*" the crucifiers!?

What's gamed in court;
is forced onto the streets. 262 *What's proven in PASS;*
is proven on the streets.

19. Cold case-in-point

{This cold case is the author's refusal to break the law and being prosecuted for refusing to break the law.}

The Cold case-in-point is the licensed author's refusal to be Accountable and Negligent of systems and superiors who compulsively corrupt and/or harm their helplessly dependent victims.

NOW comes Aaron W. Wemple, as a most legitimate member of We the People, forced into severance through no fault of his own simply trying his absolute hardest to follow the "*law*" (**Leverage) [SUFFER!]** with only dire consequences as a result.

NOW in full compliance himself with the sameness of defiance. (But without the force and trickery parts of course.)

What's gamed in court;
is forced onto the streets.   263   *What's proven in PASS;*
is proven on the streets.

THE cold case and now hot cause of
which being that Bar associated judges
and attorneys swore under oath to uphold
the People. But refuse and uphold their
own common excluding association of
members and the likes in severance from
reality instead. While using an MMD
against their own victims. And not only a
MMD, but an MMD that automatically Weegie
Wedges its helplessly dependent victims.

THE Neglect of which spreads the
witch.

NOW known to exclusively exploit
people and the People instead of
inclusively serving people and the
People.

Likewise contrasting, contrary and
tricky (their known standards and stages)
each and every judge has their "*state's*"
associate in superior clothing, strate-
gically placed with computers, internet,
programs, assistance for their legal
work, fully functional ink pens, computer
program printers for evidence, computer
program email for communication with
support, media attention, reliable and
standard mail and phone services, mail
and phone services with unsevered useable
federal regulations all on one hand.

Neglecting the other associate's hand
of the facts that people and the People

What's gamed in court;
is forced onto the streets.   264   *What's proven in PASS;*
is proven on the streets.

are handicapped and demoted (instead of upheld) on many different essential fronts. Court associates routinely neglect the facts that people are forced to compete for their lives dressed in suppressive, subjugating yellow (or other alienating color) banana looking outfit having been forced to use a suppressive, subjugating pen (ink cartridge only) preparing childish legal work, no evidence or unadulterated communications with their support, media stage set against them plus having biased any jury pool, and being forced to rely on unreliable, ever-changing, non-standard, mail and phone services. Both geared contrasting, contrary and tricky plus severed from any useable Federal Regulations.

Why not consider trying it sometime?

Why not consider equal, fair or level like they swore it's supposed to be?

Deadly Court associates are fixed up high. They obviously front Leverage as "*law*," operate in severance, sever in severance, and always say one thing but do the opposite thing. They can't help

it. That's how the supersystem is geared.
And their enforcers are forced to
follow the same exact way.

As a member of We the People I'm
fixed weakened.

The courts game is rigged. And their
judge is staged to intimidate anyone who
speaks out.

"I realized that bullying never has
to do with you. It's the bully who's
insecure."
-Shay Mitchell

Even if one of their own victims does
try to speak out no one is going to
believe a banana using a flex pen writing
childish papers all by himself. Especially when court associates uphold
themselves and their trickery so high and
mighty that they're always "*right*" and/or
Right! With literal force if need be.
That's a no-brainer.

Of course they encourage officers and
officials and even psychiatrists to
mislabel their little baby animals when
their victims are all tied up in knots
and need victimizing. They have no
choice.

What's gamed in court;
is forced onto the streets.   266   *What's proven in PASS;*
is proven on the streets.

That's how easy it is. And that's what they do.

They even go so far as to have their own victims victimized into jail, prison or a state mental health hospital if they don't fit in line with just being quit about it.

I'd be an ignorant fool too if I played their games on their board with their own rules.

And I'd be Negligent too if I did not refuse to pay taxes to support their impossible games in severance which are also illegal to defy.

Why should we pay to play these impossible games?

Especially when being upfront, fair and level is coming into focus?!

"The way to work with a bully is to take the ball and go home. First time, every time. When there's no ball, there's no game. Bullies hate that. So they'll either behave so they can play with you or they'll go bully someone else."
- Seth Godin

What's gamed in court;
is forced onto the streets.   267   *What's proven in PASS;*
is proven on the streets.

In court state statutes provide people with the right not only to proper medical treatment, but to a doctor and a psychiatrist for the defense side of offensive dependents. Not so at IDOC (Illinois Department of Corrections.)

Victims at IDOC have no doctors or psychiatrist to testify on their behalf. They're strictly at the mercy of IDOC's proxies. Not state statutes or court or humanity or sanity or even civility. They're simply shark food.

Like it's courtroom leaders make them, IDOC obviously, self-evidently and self-provingly violates state statutes, Civil Rights, Human Rights, Sane Rights and civility. All compulsively, delusioning-ly, without consciousness, without process of any sorts, and without legitimate defense of any sorts for their victims (less offensively *defensive.*") Which is simply a Suicide Sentence **CRAVING** and ending! Do you really see what witches do yet?!

Why does it look like we have a bunch of baby dictators running around all over the place casting evil spells all over and on everyone who is not detached from reality like them?

Maybe because it feels like it.

When dying feels like it to enough of us then thank God the rest of us might finally wake up.

The Fifth Amendment of the United States Constitution entitles me with the RIGHT not to implicate myself in crime.
If I paid for a bank robber to go rob a bank then wouldn't that implicate myself?

Why not stop implicating yourself?

Defiance of court orders would obviously land me in jail. So I'm forced to consider that IDOC's non-compliance to court orders and state statutes as crimes as well.
As such, I'm forced not to violate the Accountability statute. Nor do I have to constitutionally. Nor can I finan-cially.
Protecting lives from these Suicidal Traps also gives me the Right to protect myself against compulsive murderous Neglect and/or orders. Which are also state statute violations. (Although history and experience has shown that I will be punished for trying to save

What's gamed in court;
is forced onto the streets.   269   *What's proven in PASS;*
is proven on the streets.

lives.)

It is certain to say that victims of severed, self-ruling courts and IDOC will always be victimized. Especially unto death given Death's Authority who are also disorder entrepreneurs.

And especially since there are no detourant forces to stop them from being out-of-pocket.

"If you have to lie, cheat, steal, obstruct and bully to get your point across, it must not be a point capable of surviving on its own merits."
- Steven Weber

Voodoo is as voodoo does.

So, at Sound Proof we now design systems of the Light. With standards that turn light on. Protection from standards, systems and superiors that turn light off.

Why not see for yourself?

With systems of the Light you can see to protect your RIGHTS.

What's gamed in court;
is forced onto the streets.   270   *What's proven in PASS;*
is proven on the streets.

20. How systematic governments compulsively euthanize

{Systematic *"rules"* (**Rules**) [AND RULERS]
   that euthanize are the only *"answer"*
      (**Answer**) [AND *ANSWER*] today.}

Being *HYPOCRISIZED* (or worse) is the
only answer today. Which is why the new
Scientific Studies of Deathmatics and
Lifematics are so vitally important.
   The implications of Hypocrisy
Philosophies compounded with Tripolar
Court Disorders to *"protect"* (**Silence**)
them is Deathmatics.
   Deathmatics is the Scientific study
of superior pressure(s) that render
inferior death(s.)
   Deathmatics is rated on the Human
Tolerance (HT) Scale.
   Being *HYPOCRISIZED* is like

What's gamed in court;
is forced onto the streets. 271 *What's proven in PASS;*
is proven on the streets.

"*complying*" (**Impossible**)[**SUFFER!**] with courtroom practitioner's Pyramid Tripolar Disordering Device. Which is suppressive, almost unspeakably, by nature in of its self.

Being cooked *SUPERHYPOCRISIZED* is like "*defying*" (**Instinctive**) [*ONLY ONE SIDE CAN PAY SO BE QUITE AND/OR SUFFER!*] court associate's compounding Hypocrisy Philosophies. Which is permanent and perpetual, often traumatizing, pressure and persuasion all in of its self.

The more that one endures the worse the *SUPERHYPOCRISIZATION* becomes. Until the breaking point. That's the point of literal transfiguration.

Transfiguration is one final effect with multiple causes. Theoretically, and based on absolute evidence, one transfiguration effect has exactly three sustaining causes.

Protecting our most vulnerable children from being Hypocrisieced, and our most valuable institutions from Hypocrisizing is Deathmatics.

Deathmatics is measured with respect to transformation, and compounded transformations. And based on transfiguration.

Deathmatics looks at pressured and/or persuaded life changes and intolerable life changing causes.

Superior pressure drives unpressurizing motives.

We need to learn how much air they can push into the tire before the tire blows. (Likewise for those tricking the air out.)

Making the strong stronger while neglecting the weak to be weaker is a sure way to deflate all of the tires at the same time easier and easier.

In other words, the air's leaking out all on its own and nobody knows how to find the holes except those who are blown out already.

So why not patch the tires left with holes in them? You can't make them new again. But can protect newer tires from getting holes.

What's gamed in court;
is forced onto the streets.   273   *What's proven in PASS;*
is proven on the streets.

What's gamed in court;
is forced onto the streets.

What's proven in PASS;
is proven on the streets.

The Rule of Slip Knots: "*Bullies*" and/or Bullies *figuratively* and/or **Literally** stick their victims *VICTIMIZED*.

Bullyism is as bullyism does. Why wouldn't superior reports instinctively suppress inferiors while building themselves up at the same time?

Becoming **Systematically Euthanized**, or finally transfigured, is simply "*trying*" until the bitter end to accept system(s) and their superior(s) that are themselves and/or together impossible to comply with and wrong to defy. Which compulsively compounds the inherent consequences only to their victims the more systems and the more superiors that they're subject to, and the more that those systems and superiors contrast each other.

What's gamed in court;
is forced onto the streets.

What's proven in PASS;
is proven on the streets.

<u>The Rule of Thumb Knots:</u> The chain of command rules that not only oppose each other, but contrast their victims likewise, dishearten and render their victimized victims unable to follow impossible to follow rules and orders that are illegal to defy even if they were possible to follow.

What's gamed in court;
is forced onto the streets.

What's proven in PASS;
is proven on the streets.

Being Hypocrisized, Superhyocrisized, Systematically Euthanized and/or Systematically Kidnapped ultimately has to follow exclusively licensed Bar-Courts. Bar associates who are now known to be detached from reality and severing in severance themselves.

It's enforced as illegal not to follow them. Yet it's impossible for anyone else to.

Experimentally, the only thing that is legal and that is possible and that is compliant with them in court is **death.** Which fits perfectly in line with Death's Authority. (Which is premeditated of course.)

Everyone has to live up to what court(s) expect. Even if they are legitimately and figuratively Death's Authority. If we don't then we can and will be found guilty in a court of "*law*" (**Leverage.)** Which is disordering and/or a trap in of its self.

It's enforced as illegal not to live up to what court counselors expect.

Of course outside systems and super-iors have to follow suit. And of course people and the People are likewise rendered irrelevant and/or "*worse.*" Job security is impulsive.

You, me and everyone else can and

What's gamed in court;
is forced onto the streets.   279   *What's proven in PASS;*
is proven on the streets.

will be found "*guilty*" and/or Guilty by
Leverage hidden from us. Hidden Leverage
that absolutely violates humanity, sanity, our most vulnerable children, and
our most valuable institutions alike.
That's **JUSTICE** and/or "*justice*" today.
 Which actually feels like permanent
and perpetual **HATE**.

 Enemy-ism is as enemy-ism does.

 Why not protection?

What's gamed in court;
is forced onto the streets.　　280　　*What's proven in PASS;*
is proven on the streets.

Discovering why Life Matters

Like most of us, I used to believe "*law*" but always felt the pressures of "*hidden*" (**Leverage.**) When I should've magically been aware of Leverage and ignored "*law.*"

Courts contrasting reality is not only neglected, and not only taught, but it is enforced.

Why enlighten the people when we're so much easier to take advantage of by keeping the light off?

Being forced to be subject to Hypocrisy alone is mad & absolutely maddening. Especially being forced to depend on multiple impossible Hypocrisies. My best friend shot himself because he was impossibly & unspeakably Super-hypocrisized.

Mentally pressured children who are victimized victims of bullies have been known to do the same.

I've seen plenty of children from court "*order*" suicidal.

I've been to prison for following State Statutes & refusing to violate laws.

I've had my children Systematically

Kidnapped and left with no way of turning on the light.

I was impotent against it because I couldn't have known the "*law*" (**Leverage**) twisting game. I was taught better.

In Science Law means absolute. And Leverage means Leverage. Law can never legitimately mean Leverage!

Being Hypocrisized, Superhypocrisized, Systematically Kidnapped & Systematically Euthanized absolutely "*complies*" (**defies) [*SUFFER FROM*]** judicial supersuperiors orchestrating superiors versus inferiors. Strictly offensive report forms (like VA hospitals, DOC, police, etc.) for evidence with duplicates, distribution & publishing plus dependent superior inferiorated inferior "*versus*" offensively "*defensive*" reports. It's a one-sided system over like-wise systems. And that's a no-brainer. Which gives not only motive for the dumbing-down of America, but cause as well.

Satan, I've found your weapon!

For most attorneys the Hypocrisy Philosophy that's enforced contrastingly is a well paved golden path to the top.

For example, I'm routinely "*spun*" dictatively just to posture & pay one of

What's gamed in court;
is forced onto the streets.
282
What's proven in PASS;
is proven on the streets.

them.

Why wouldn't reports reflect them at their own victim's expense?

For most psychiatrists, it's a golden goose to **SHRINK** victims. For example, I'm routinely **SHRUNK** by a psychiatrist so that superior report form evidence & a witness are in favor of my opponents.

Why wouldn't reports reflect selfish posture at their patients expense?

For most officers this is justified and/or "*justified*" Bullyism.

For most officials, its Neglect and "*neglect*" on one hand and Benefits and "*benefits*" on the other hand while stuffing support into both of their pockets with no hands.

For people & the People, it's suppression and/or traumatization swindling jewels for the Crown of Hypocrisy.

Nobody really cares or acknowledges the estimated 27.6 million victimized victims who have fallen in the line of "*duty*" (**Duty)** [**DUTY!**] so far.

"Just take your lumps and shut up," I can still hear them say.

For those exclusive associates in court with political ambitions (and some elected jobs have to be exclusive associates) it "*works*" (**Hedges**) [*SUFFER*] like a charm that's illegal not to believe from the county courthouse all the way to the White House.

For example, now that I know that I know better, I'm routinely "*spun*," **SHRUNK** & publicly published against by & for supersuperiors who commonly "*profess*" (**Switch**), practice, uphold & then enforce "*hiding*" (**Leverage**) Hedging "*law*" (**Leverage**) [*SUPERHYPOCRISIZING VICTIM!*]

All because I practice real, absolute scientific Law. Which upholds its self. And you and everyone else can always see it and count on it. It's foolproof. It soundproofs systems and/or superiors. It's impossible to fail. It eliminates setting other people up to fail just so that the setter-uppers win.

But a scientific caliber of intellect is outside of their "*schemes*" (**Regimes**) of things. So it's forced to be subject to counterintelligence while they're in control. In essence, it's worse than criminal today.

If somebody, anybody would have at least warned me that courts really practice, uphold & enforce Leverage instead of Law then my children could have had a father in their lives. And my life would not have been ruined. And my best friend & many other helplessly dependent, compulsively victimized victims would still be alive. And all of their children would have had that parent in their lives. And many children could have found comfort in the arms of their fathers. And many soldiers would not have fought and died in vain. And so many people would not have to be fighting through so many virtually impossible, illegal to defy stigmas, dogmas, enigmas, detached superiors & supersuperiors, and detached systems & supersystems.

All of which renders all authority & no responsibility for themselves while neglecting us into hell.

In reality, there's nothing worse than for men, women & children alike to be spun, shrunk, tie-up, torture & neglect permanently and perpetually forever by severed supermen needing helplessly dependent inferior victims just to "*justify*" themselves being detached from reality.

And in reality, when there's no

What's gamed in court;
is forced onto the streets.   285   *What's proven in PASS;*
is proven on the streets.

chance or choice because it's illegal not to comply but it's also impossible to comply, and it doesn't matter if you're disabled because they disabled you, or that you know better because you earned it, just comply with the impossible or else you're a criminal!

This type of ordered severance, known to pressure only one direction – supersuperiors-to-superiors-to-inferiors – is known to be a Suicidal Sentence **_CRAVING_** an ending for the foot stools. Regardless of who cast the bait, or who holds the line on the traps.

Courts, like prisons, know this. They use this. They know what perpetual pressure does. They know what the perpetual pressure that might need some "_persuasion_" does.

In the book, "Winning Human Authority," page 188, a Texas judge threatened school children saying, "Anybody …, no kidding, is going to wish he or she had died as a child when this court gets through with it." - 171 F.3d 1013 Doe v. Santa Fe Independent School District, Galveston, TX 1999.

They know this. And it's simple to instigate a helpless dependent or dependents just to victimize them.

It's cruel and it's unusual to us.

What's gamed in court;
is forced onto the streets.   286   _What's proven in PASS;_
is proven on the streets.

But, as it turns out, leading by misleading detached from reality is infinitely lucrative & infinitely subject-able. Which is perfect for political & price fixing.

Political & price fixing using hidden weapons culminating in a literal nutshell if it comes to that. Which is home for some.

But a firewall of Hypocrisy is far from Democracy.

With all authority & no responsibility, leading by misleading is, above all, non-binding. Nothing sticks but crooking others in court.

Men, women & children are forced to "*follow*" (**Impossible)** [*SUFFER*] these terms of their trade.

But supersuperiors do it of their own free will. Knowing full well the well paved golden path of both financial & political advantages that are fixed for them inside of the Weegie Wedge.

We the People can't even approach getting started healing Hypocrisy wounds with True Democracy as is.

If not in denial, liability and shame prohibits the truth from ever being exposed by those culpable.

They can and will dig us in deeper and deeper to just keep themselves floating.

So, since severance is likewise compliance & defiance, why not join a fresh start? That's the Upright USA Race Family Matters Mission.

It makes no sense in the real world that impossible to comply with "*laws*" (**Leverages) [*SUFFERANCE*]** dictates decisions. Because we are all just destroying ourselves buying into "*tasty*" (**Tyranny.)**

For example, ever wonder who's winning that war on "*drugs*?" Drugs are because the **ABUSED** and the **Abusers** are beating themselves & each other up being subject to impossible to follow Hypocrisy Philosophies.

While promoters have already set themselves up both financially & politically. And they're long gone.

As proof of terroristic "*wars*," drugs now take the highest promotional stage while most people & People are down & out.

This is due to upholding the RDRP (Rope-a-Dope & Ride Piggyback) practices and/or operations.

What's gamed in court;
is forced onto the streets.   288   *What's proven in PASS;*
is proven on the streets.

Detached Hovering Eyes swell well by and for ordering bricks & mortar shrunk into Hell.

Only true bullies would even engage in a war where their enemies have to be their own subjects.

"Agree with me or I'll punish you!"

That in of its self is a fixed war.

Supersuperiors treat every other country better than they treat their own kin. At least in other countries inferiors can get some of our promoters attention when they're committing Genocide.

Yet, even bullies are trapped faced with liability issues holding them hostage to ever stop these delusioning wars now.

Like slaves to a master are inferiors played by & for supersuperior's game. Then trapped in the device and its left over vices and/or vises.

One may "wish" but never truly fix irreparable damages.

Which is the game victims have to play "*trying*" to appease undeniable & impossible courts. It's routine.

What's gamed in court;
is forced onto the streets.
289
What's proven in PASS;
is proven on the streets.

A game compounded compulsively given premeditated published offensive superior "*freedom of the press*" reports which always trump impossible & unspeakably defenseless inferior-ated Free Speech in court. (Therefore, the only things that judicially has to matter on the streets.)

As the head VA hospital psychiatrist who was demoted for caring about people instead of sticking together for the system said on Channel 5 St. Louis News, "There's an insatiable need to look good on paper."

Dare I say, "duh."

Without reports people & the People are less than invisible to the courts, hence the streets. This common court "*order*" is enforced to be contagious. And with either compliance or defiance we're Permanently Perpetually Negatively Compounded Leveraged Compulsively (PPNCLC), hence reality.

In the real world where's the bottleneck in the systems? Where are caring systems & healing people with good intentions compromised and handicapped counter intelligently and rendered null, void and/or "*worse*" (with force if need be?)

What's gamed in court;
is forced onto the streets.　　290　　*What's proven in PASS;*
is proven on the streets.

There's is literally Hypocrisizing their own victims & systems. Or "*tasty*" (**TYRANIZATION.**)

Mine is literally True Democracies. Or Healing Freedomizations.

Scientific Spot Trials (and Scientific Trials Live) are not a trap that they would require bait. Nor a Death Trap that they would require permanent and perpetual excuses.

Human Authorities are not contrasting, contrary or tricky. Human Authorities are, well, human authorities.

How much better will it be to have Spot Trials instantly online when we can instead of delayed detached pressure burdening everyone financially, physically, mentally & emotionally from the games people have to play just to compete?

We could actually learn, improve & heal some rather than unlearn, disprove & hurt all.

Being **Hypocrisized** is the State of many children from Family Court today.
Being **Superhypocrisized** is the State

What's gamed in court;
is forced onto the streets.　　291　　*What's proven in PASS;*
is proven on the streets.

of many dependents of pressurized "*con-victions*" (**Submissions.)**

Being *Systematically Euthanized* is the only viable ending for many helpless dependents victimized compulsively by courts, jails, prisons, VA hospitals, orphanages, nursing homes & other contrasting, contrary & tricky systems and/or superiors.

As is, "*schemes*" (**Regimes)** gain both money & power by elevating Hypocrisy while neglecting & rendering people and the People null, void and/or "*worse.*"

And due to liability, this is a one direction train ride that can only accelerate into the oblivion. It cannot decelerate.

My Race Mission in life is to protect even the supersuperior's children from being Hypocrisized or worse.

Studying Deathmatics & Lifematics scientifically will accomplish that and much more while engineering governments with scientific standards through human authority.

If there are any impossibilities we'll know it automatically. We won't have to wait until tires blow out and the masses wake up before we start to care for our tires.

Please pray that our children & their children will stop being Hypocrisized and start being truthenized.

And please pray that True Democracy will be given the platform that it deserves (level) to help heal the wounds caused by Hypocrisy Philosophies.

And please pray that Scientific Trials, even Spot Trials Live, can and will add that much needed, rightful & justifiable human element.

The human element that is now enforced to be null, void and/or "worse" (PPNCLC.)

But the old way and the new way cannot relate only deviate.

The implications of True Democracies with Scientific Standards, Human

Principles and Sane Order to protect them is Lifematics. That's where we should go.

All together rendering True Law Anew.

True Law Anew that can & will re-engineer systems & superiors from the ground up.

That's Winning Human Authority.

And Winning Human Authority by the Lord's Cup renders expert experience.

Add Science, and that's a game-changer.

Why not be the winning team again?

<u>The Rules of Working Thumbs</u>: Kindly consider words that edify. Not words that crucify. Especially in leading positions. And especially behind closed doors. Where "*anything*" and "*everything*" can be made unconsciously to fit. And super especially when enforced instinctively to be made to fit.

   Edify, don't crucify.

What's gamed in court;
is forced onto the streets.   295   *What's proven in PASS;*
is proven on the streets.

21. The compulsive 21st Century Crucifixion

The compulsive 21st Century Crucifixion is impossible compliance that's also illegal to defy.

This primarily unconscious crucifixion is from intellectual slip knoters authorizing all of the Rule, rules and rulers.

Why not loosen the ropes? Let the good ponies out and run for a while? Or at least crack a window. It's suffocating down here in the vile!

Like the Bar's court, signing IDOC's exit agreement self-evidently violated Illinois State Statutes. This again has proven to be the routine.

Though if I don't "*comply*" with orders that trap me in violation then it's known that I will go to seg. (a segregation cell.)

Number one on IDOC's exit agreements (from the parole class booklets at the time) was that I cannot violate Illinois State Statutes.

And I obviously already know that compliance with even the littlest of the sameness of defiance is much worse than a crime. Or else I wouldn't be in prison for refusing to violate the law, corruption and humanity.

I know that the United States Constitution Bill of Rights untouchably (without an Amendment – which is available for exercise) ORDERS that **all** cases equal a Democratic **jury** Rule (Amendment VI.) That those two RIGHTS cannot be **denied**, **construed to be denied** or **abridged** (Amendment XIV.)

I also know that Conspiring against (US Constitutional) Civil Rights is a violation of Illinois State Statute 725 ILCS 5/8-21.

And I also know that Neglect is a violation.

So compliance to number one on IDOC's exit agreement is wittingly impossible.

I know that IDOC obviously, self-evidently and self-provingly violates Illinois State Statutes.

I know that I can't go into a bank with a bank robber without being Accountable.

I'm currently in prison for refusing to violate these State Statutes, US Constitutional Rights and even the court clerk's exclusive brand of practitioners being upheld.

So what should I do? Stay trapped in prison for following the law?

Or should I just give in and fully comply with the "*law*" (Leverage) and sever other people while in severance myself instead?

Or should I just Neglect it and hope that it all just "*magically*" (Impossible) disappears?!

But this is obviously a death sentence **CRAVING** an ending!

Enough crying. Let's get real and get over these problems already.

IDOC's number one exit agreement condition not to violate Illinois State Statutes must obviously be a trick or a trap to entrap victims into violation. (And that also fits the pattern of state statute violating, corrupting and abusing that's being upheld.)

Thus, if it is a trick then it can carry no real weight.

And if it is a trap then it's a crime to trick signers into signing themselves into violation.

Even if IDOC's agreements were not a joke or a crime, it is not possibly mutually beneficial to sign a contract when one party's life depends on the other party.

We all know that masters can prime, pressure, paint and then seal to exploit their own helplessly dependent victims just to be victimized.

THEREFORE, in full compliance with 21st Century Crucifixion (the sameness of divisional defiance - without the force and trickery parts of course), signing supersystem and/or supersuperior agreements while helplessly dependent on them obviously violates State Statutes, Equal Protection Rights and is sealed to be used against me in a court of "*law*" (Leverage) without so much as a Miranda Right warning me of as much.

WHAT THE FLIP IS THE POINT OF LIVING WHEN SUPPRESSION AND/OR TRAUMATIZATION IS

THE COMPULSIVE RULE OF THUMB KNOTS ENFORCED TODAY!?

At least criminals get know their Miranda Rights. At least they're advised that anything that they say can and will be used against them in a court of "*law*" (Leverage.)

Not so much with non-criminals. We have to find out the hard way.

When the crooked owns the rule, and only the straight are neglected as a tool, then you know you've gone too far; You've gone full circle like a fool.

22. Hot cause-on-point

{The hot cause from courtroom
practitioners severing in severance is to
likewise sever from their severance.}

Regarding IDOC Prison Review Board
Order for me dated January 7, 2014, in
the sameness of severing in severance,
the Prison Review Board Order did not
even make it possible to comply with
court Orders. Let alone Civil Rights,
State Statutes or even reality.

Severing in severance upheld;
Must be trickled down;
The fooled stay stuck on gold;
So silver tongues drip to the ground.

In full compliance with the court
practitioners defiance, the IDOC Prison
Review Board Ordered "*something impos-*

What's gamed in court;
is forced onto the streets.   303   *What's proven in PASS;*
is proven on the streets.

sible and obviously irrelevant."

I never saw these people. And they never saw me.

However, I did try to follow their impossible to follow Orders and was put back into jail for trying.

Not that facts even have to matter for additional punishments to be handed down by additional systems and additional superiors obviously operating in severance themselves, but IDOC is well-known to be a proxy (agent) of the courts.

The courts are not supposed to be a proxy to IDOC. Nor especially out on its own out in never ending never never land somewhere with no boundaries. It's no wonder that nobody can comply. It's no wonder that, *"it's job security,"* is their common excuse.

And especially with infinite figurative *"bullyism"* plus infinite literal Bullyism at their disposal. It makes it just fun and games for them.

Yet IDOC and the likes enforce as much without Due Process, a defense or even the reality of their own victims taken into consideration.

IDOC Orders routinely do not comply with court Orders. And often they impossibly contradict one another. Leaving their victims inherently stranded victimized by multiple agencies without legitimate, unbiased and unliable recourse.

IDOC, like courtroom practices and the likes, are outside of any boundaries enforcing their own severed delusions off into never ending never never land somewhere adding boundaries and punishments themselves onto their own victim's already broken backs. All at whim and in full compliance with the sameness of defying court Orders, State Statutes, Civil Rights, Processes of any sorts and their victims own realities.

Compulsive condemnations of this sort being obviously detached from reality are way out of control. And based solely on delusions.

People are dying in reality.

But jobs detached from reality are secure.

The sometimes impossible to follow vexes by & for other detached people's vices force self-destruction on their stranded and invisible helplessly dependent victims just to *"comply"* (**Impossible**) [*INHERENTLY SUPPRESSED AND/OR TRAUMATIZED!*]

For example, those of us in prison who were previously prescribed simple chronic medical items were not only physically victimized over and over and over and over again for as much (until we finally have to kill ourselves just to get relief, and/or instinctively lash-out) but with being intellectually "*toyed*" with on systematic forms by superior medical reports to skirt liability.

Which renders doctors pointless and patients "*worse*" than mute.

And having my life ruined and my children scarred forever just for upholding the law just doesn't add up.

Based solely on delusional authority the 3rd Reich did the same things.

Like many severed systems and their severed systematic superiors, doctors and psychiatrists at IDOC are known to protect IDOC at the expense of their patients.

Systems forced into operating by severing in severance are known to protect themselves at the expense and suffering of people. Often giving the excuse, "*its policy.*" Or worse, "*that it's job security!*"

But their excuses equal other people's abuses.

Like many victims, my chronic medical conditions were routinely violated. And I am routinely victimized to this day simply because I am disabled.

And I am disabled because they disabled me.

Do you "*see*" or **SEE** the pattern here?

This is all from Death Authorities unquestionable Death Trap!

And efforts to report these crimes were and are to this day not only routinely obstructed, but worse, also routinely neglected.

But all of which are chronically felt with unspeakable, uncorrectable, permanent and perpetual pain, expense and sufferance.

Why not at least check the air in the tires?

What's gamed in court;
is forced onto the streets.

What's proven in PASS;
is proven on the streets.

Dimming the Lights

    The only thing worse than having
obstacles to get over;
    Is having tricky distractions to get
around;

    Obstacles are easy to see;
    But distractions are impossible to
"*see*";

    Obstacles you know you can feel;
    But distractions you don't know you
will feel;

    And tricky distractions come in like
"*we're doing you a favor!*"
    So it makes no sense that they might
get in the way to eventually butcher you
in the back.

What's gamed in court;
is forced onto the streets.   309   *What's proven in PASS;*
is proven on the streets.

Brightening the Light

What's your goal?
What do you care about?

Now that, that should stay;
But be careful though, it could be
used against you in a court of "*law*"
(Leverage) for play;

Look at the Lord;
Now he's a light that can only shine;

All others try to stand;
But His, they won't be denied;

So the Lord, He's untouchable;
We serve His words on a platinum
platter;

Ahhh....those little dimming devils;
On their own they don't even matter!

What's gamed in court;
is forced onto the streets.   311   *What's proven in PASS;*
is proven on the streets.

When the highest and the broadest perceived "*authorities*" over the land benefits themselves with respect to the ills of society, then both the healthy and the ills of society are forced to follow suit. That's a Death Spiral.

After all, isn't it enforced as illegal not to be this way?

That's the exclusive courtroom's contradictions compared to reality. And that's solely on them.

The only variables in a Death Spiral are the intensity and duration. Which is how deep we are down in it.

It doesn't matter which side you're on. Both sides down in the Death Spiral feel its affects.

But none of us should be responsible for the lack of knowledge. Or for other practices mistakes.

What's gamed in court;
is forced onto the streets.   313   *What's proven in PASS;*
is proven on the streets.

Concentrated, the Hovering Eyes in a three point stance over the drain of society compels the speed of the drain for the police against the people underneath of them.

While being in severance through no fault of our own, the People and the police cannot compel the Eye of these storms unless the Hovering Eyes are willing.

Therein lays the deadlock. Therein amplifies the storm.

Therein lies the quagmire that I go to prison for trying to solve.

It turns out that the crafty little judicial Death Trap posing as "*justice*" is really just a Catch-22 Device forcing and enforcing Catch-22 figurative vices and literal vises all over the place which prescribe vexes on all of their helplessly dependent victims.

Where vexed victims are intellectually bound hopeless and/or physically bound helpless.

Vexed victims are damned if they do comply with the pyramid scheme and damned even worse if they don't comply with the scheme.

"Most assuredly, I say to you, he who
does not enter the sheepfold by the door,
but climbs up some other way, the same is
a thief and a robber."
– Jesus

The inherent consequences from all
judicial benefactors who are now known to
divide by rooting in "*hiding*" (Leverage)
is that officers and officials are left
leading by misleading. While people and
the People are simply neglected stuck
severed to suffer unspeakably and to pay
unconditionally.

This Ultimate Judicial Enigma (UJE)
protects the known Crown of Hypocrisy
instead of the People.
An ultimate quagmire to now get out
of.
An ultimate dilemma for swelled heads
to now level with.
But a mind boggling and/or body
boggling conflicting, confusing conundrum
to experience.

It sucks!

What's gamed in court;
is forced onto the streets.   315   *What's proven in PASS;*
is proven on the streets.

Overall, a very expensive, very painful and very pointless psychological-to-physical holocaust needlessly.

That's Hypocrisy Philosophies at the wheel.

And that's "*law*" (**Leverage**) [*SUFFER!*] regardless growing today.

When the cause of many problems is right there in front and you choose to neglect it and look the other way, then it is on you when it betrays your own children. And when it forces them to stray.

To get butchered in the back or to walk off of the plank at gun point? Now there's a scenario that some of us see every day. While the rest? Well, they have to look away.

23. In full compliance with the sameness of defiance

{Answer to Solicitation for Violations.}

The United States of America?!

Aaron W. Wemple's Uniting Practice

vs.

Bar Associates Dividing Practice Being Upheld

(Re. Montgomery Co., IL Clerks "Case number: 12-CF-178")

What's gamed in court;
is forced onto the streets.　　317　　*What's proven in PASS;*
is proven on the streets.

ANSWER TO SOLICITATION FOR STATE STATUTE
& OTHER VIOLATIONS

On July 12, 2014 I received a notice from the Montgomery County, IL Circuit Clerk that there is now a *"Status Hearing"* in case number 12-CF-178. Well after the facts. And well after having suffered from the inherent consequences of many systems figuratively and literally severing me in severance.

In regard to the notice from unauthorized Circuit Clerk to be Statutorily Accountable and Statutorily Negligent of proven violations, proven corrupting and proven abusing, I thanked her for the invitation.

But I respectfully declined. I asked the clerk to "please do not have your bullies physically beat me up! Or have your psychiatrists intellectually 'beat me up!' You know for sure now that I will follow the law either way."

I mean, I went to prison for following the law (state statutes, the US Constitution, the IL Constitution , each judges and attorney's own oaths, and even their own severance alike.) Why would I start violating these Laws now? It's not even my fault that compliance is

What's gamed in court;
is forced onto the streets.   318   *What's proven in PASS;*
is proven on the streets.

impossible! (Yet enforced either way - whether followed or not.)

Plus I seem to be the only one trying to fix these obvious problems now that we all know their obvious compulsive consequences.

I couldn't even drive to her Statues Hearing if I wanted to. If they see me on the road then they always pull me over and make up some crazy "*story*" on their formal report form evidence. And I'm always found guilty in their crazy "*court*" whether I conspire with its obvious fraud or not.

And I know that the clerk's Bullies and "*bullies*" can and will drive to come and see me either way. They've proven that. They did it when I was pressed and painted in jail like an animal and then sealed me in writing that way. Why shouldn't they come to their own victim's house instead of the other way around? That's only fair.

So I remain in full compliance with this courthouse's brand of defiance. And the clerk's brand of judge and associates can either accept my public deceleration of independence and keep the house and the truck and the career that they've stolen and let it go at that, or not and we'll keep fighting for the future of all

What's gamed in court;
is forced onto the streets.   319   *What's proven in PASS;*
is proven on the streets.

mankind. But I'd leave that ball in their court.

But you (the clerk) know that they and I are at an impasse because of the crimes that they've self-evidently committed against me. And I've paid for their mistakes over and over and over and over and over again. And I'm through. I've drawn the line. And showed you where it's at. And begged you to stop crossing it.

Why would I jeopardize the truth when error is all that they have left going for them? I'm good regardless. I can't mess with them. I won't mess with them.

You have to know by now that they do have others push unsuspecting people too hard, and have others persuade too well. And you have to know by now that they are the ones obviously detached from reality. And that nobody else is going to stop them the More and the "more" carried away from reality that they get. That's a well-known, undeniable trend. Now known to be Enforced and/or "authorized" in total disregard of other people's careers and other people's humanity.

And the more that they drift away out in never ending never never land somewhere the worse others are forced to become.

So this is even for their own good. How mad are people going to be when they find out that they were played like a fool just to be stabbed in the back?

And they already have others push and persuade their own victims into being victimized beyond the point of death before they ever even consider accepting any responsibility for their own actions.

I've told the clerk before that I'm done paying for their mistakes. They've had a choice all along. They've had a choice their whole careers whether or not to mislead people from their own disenfranchised vantage points detached from reality.

But I have never had the choice. I was forced into this sick flippin' mess. So I'm done with their brand of violating, corrupting and harming. It does less than no good to those who've never hurt anybody.

So why not fix what's obviously broke and needlessly breaking people?

Now, for those who have hurt other people, fine, go ahead and throw all the Crazy and "crazy" that you want at them. I'm on board with an eye for an eye.

But for people who have never hurt

What's gamed in court;
is forced onto the streets.   321   *What's proven in PASS;*
is proven on the streets.

anybody else in their entire lives this "*process*" (Pain and Suffering) doesn't even fit true criminals.

So if they try to kill me some more for them being detached from reality then that's now on the clerks.

I'm going to die with my boots on either way. Standing up for the law, state statutes, my Rights, humanity, sanity and the future of all mankind.

If the clerk wants to help them violate me for refusing to let them violate, corrupt and hurt other jobs and other people then that's on the court clerks now.

I'm all in until the end having lost everything and everyone anyway.

Just please warn the police. They are the court practitioner's victims too. Neither of us should be Ordered into crossfire.

It would be a shame to see victims die at the hands of other victims. Because that would still leave the true criminals up in the hot air on top. And it would leave the clerks a close second.

The court's dividing practice that's upheld today is now known to corrupt other people's professions and to both figuratively and physically murder other people. And I will not be any party to

---

that.

Good riddance either way.
Aaron W. Wemple

(Unfortunately, the circuit clerk must not have accepted that she trapped me into violation because she then put out a hit on me.)

The Law Doctor

*What's gamed in court;
is forced onto the streets.*

324

*What's proven in PASS;
is proven on the streets.*

THE UPRIGHT UNITED STATES OF AMERICA RACE AND FAMILY MATTERS MISSION

{Answer to Clerk Plotting Victims Murder.}

The United States of America?!

Aaron W. Wemple's Uniting Practice

vs.

Bar Associates Dividing Practice Being Upheld

(Clerks "Case number: 12-CF-178")

MOTION FOR THE ACCUSED TO STOP ORDERING THEIR VICTIM FIXED IN VIOLATION AND/OR PLOTTING HIS MURDER

NOW comes Aaron W. Wemple, victimized victim, to beg for a civilizing resolution with his abusers, reporting that:

Unauthorized Circuit Clerk Holly Lemons, who is now known to set-up victims for the State Bar Associates (who are now known to violate Illinois State Statutes, Corrupting and Assaulting their own victims) to be victimized is being accused of plotting Aaron W. Wemple's murder.

At approximately 12:20 pm on Wednesday July 23, 2014 the perpetually victimized victim, Aaron W. Wemple, received a phone call from James at the DCRM homeless shelter and halfway house in Decatur, IL. James informed Aaron that there was a letter there from the Montgomery County Courthouse.

The last letter that Aaron received from the Montgomery County Courthouse on July 12, 2014 was at the correct address in Edwardsville, IL.

Mr. Wemple's "ANSWER..." to the last letter that he legitimately received was mailed to Montgomery County Circuit Clerk Holly Lemons on July 14, 2014. In that "ANSWER TO SOLICITATION TO VIOLATE IL STATE STATUTES, CORRUPTION & HUMANITY," Aaron wrote:

"Please do not have your bullies physically beat me up. Or have your psychiatrists mentally '*beat me up*.' You know for sure now that I will follow the law either way."

What's gamed in court;
is forced onto the streets.   326   *What's proven in PASS;*
is proven on the streets.

"...I went to prison for following the law..."

"It is not my fault that compliance is impossible."

"If they see me then they always pull me over and make up some '*story*' on their reports..."

"You know that they and I are at an impasse because of their crimes against me..."

"You have to know by now that they do have others push their victims too hard and/or have others persuade their victims too well."

"I have told you before that I am done paying for their mistakes. They have had a choice all along....But I have not."

"So if they try to kill me some more for them being detached from reality then that's now on you."

"I'm going to die with my boots on. Standing up for the law..."

"Just please warn the police. They

are court practitioners divided victims
too. And it will be a shame to see
victims and victims die at the hands of
one another. Because that would still
leave the true criminals up in the hot
air on top. And the clerks a close second
right behind them."

The now known but Neglected
victimized victim cannot by any sane
means be held liable for mail sent to
addresses that he has never specifically
given to the court associates.

This is obviously evidence of deadly
plot.

Wittingness exists that everyone
will accept that a warrant is okay to be
issued if I do not abide by Notice to
appear. (Whether pertinent evidence is
neglected or not.) And whether or not
that warrant results in casualties or
not. Death after the facts is still death
after the facts.

However, this now routine pattern of
wittingly victimizing the victim (280
times now) fits in line perfectly with
the accused establishment.

Any warrant issued as a result of
the games that judicial practitioners are
known to play will be met with humble
forgiveness.

What's gamed in court;
is forced onto the streets.   328   *What's proven in PASS;*
is proven on the streets.

The accused have always had a choice.

Their victims have not.

Maybe it's time to at least consider alternatives?

WHEREFORE, the permanently and perpetually victimized victim Motions the Accused and their Circuit Clerk Associate to sit down upfront, fair and level and reason out this cold case and now hot cause towards understanding like civilized adults. Instead of plotting their own victim's murder behind his back like uncivilized little children.

May God bless you & yours,
Aaron W. Wemple
Author & Engineer of *I R Physics*
Clean Law Union
Now designing systems upright
(After dyeing from systems down-low)

"Resurrection from the 21st Century Crucifixion"

What's gamed in court;
is forced onto the streets.   329   *What's proven in PASS;*
is proven on the streets.

24. The end of an era

{The final result of old JOP (Judicial Operating Procedure.)}

On October 3, 2013 I was at the IDOC "*law*" library to have some copies made by an IDOC employee to fit my Appeal requirements when the employee took my evidence, tampered with it, obstructed my process and had the audacity to write me a ticket. All for simply trying to follow court Order (which is now known the legitimate way to contradict IDOC rules.)

In her offensively "*defensive*" systematic superior report form evidence she made an excuse that protected her at my expense.

On October 8, 2013 I was called to an adjustment committee so that they could tell me if I was guilty or not innocent of the violation.

I said that, "I wish to follow the law and report the crime of tampering with evidence and Obstruction of Process. I at least need to replace the missing evidence with a police report for court. And because there is no consequences for IDOC employees sabotaging other peoples Appeal."

But the officer kicked me out of the office because I tried to protect myself instead of just lying down and accepting being their victimized victim.

THIS IS ROUTINE!

He put me on C-grade for defending myself. Which meant that I could not buy the much needed food from the commissary for all of those times when I couldn't walk over to the chow hall because of the pain and suffering from their medical neglect. And from disabilities that where my fault for "*trying*" (**Impossible**) [*DIE!*] following the law.

It was known that I was trying to press charges against their doctor for criminal Neglect. It was well known that he routinely neglected mine and many other people's obvious disabilities and "*mislabeled*" them with something else.

Two helplessly dependent victims died while I was there. This was "*routine.*" This is ***ROUTINE!***

It is becoming well known that matters like these are ignored, covered up and/or made "*worse*" for trying to fix them.

Bringing these matters to light is avoided at all costs to others.

The epitome of bullyism is when it's worse than a crime to follow the law. When it's worse than a crime to go to the doctors for a disability or for chronic pain and suffering. And it's worse than a crime to go to a counselor for help dealing with the emotional corrupting and harming that's done needlessly.

And it's been proven that IDOC and Illinois Courts alike are willing to let their victims die due to systematic errors. I just wish that they would find a more humane way of murdering us.

This routine pattern of JOP (now scientifically proven to be by & for Bar associates ruling courts and beyond contrasting, contrary and tricky supreme) makes it impossible to follow the law, to follow mixed orders, or to follow severed orders.

Which is <u>exactly</u> like Bar associates swearing under oath that it's the law to follow the United States Constitution. But in reality it's much, much, much Worse <u>and/or</u> "*worse*" than a crime!

What's gamed in court;
is forced onto the streets.   333   *What's proven in PASS;*
is proven on the streets.

It's not even my fault that it's impossible to follow the law! And why's it my permanent & perpetual fault that it's worse than a crime to even try?! It's not. Only the inherent consequences are.

That's having been set up to fail. And it can only come from the top-down.

Those of us underneath of these Catch-22 Authorities and/or *"authorities"* (damned if we don't and damned even worse of we do) eventually just have to lay down and die. That's the final results of JOP protecting the MMD with Weegie Wedging Magic.

While those above of these Catch-22 Authorities and *"authorities"* are blessed if we don't and blessed even more if we do. That's having been set up to succeed. And it can only come from the top-down.

What's bass-ackwards got to do with anything? Everything?

It is a counterintuitive system from the top-down. After all, does it really make any sense that the farther away from a problem that one gets that the better the decision is? No. It does not.

It makes less than zero sense that the farther you get away from a problem to the highest court with ten literal degrees of separation from reality by then that it's a "*superior*" decision!

That's crazy!

A legitimate Superior decision would be on the spot, ground level, face-to-face, stuck in reality.

Not up in the clouds delusioning others to make it "fit" and/or FIT!!!

What's gamed in court;
is forced onto the streets.
335
What's proven in PASS;
is proven on the streets.

"...because they refused to love the truth and so be saved. Therefore God sends them a strong delusion, so that they may believe what is false, in order that all may be condemned who do not believe the truth but had pleasure in unrighteousness."
   - *2 Thessalonians 2:11-12*

"It is far better to grasp the universe as it really is than to persist in delusion, however satisfying and reassuring."
   - *Carl Sagan*

What's gamed in court;
is forced onto the streets.   336   *What's proven in PASS;*
is proven on the streets.

25. Casting call for Truth in Justice Actors for a Scientific Universe

Scientifically, severing courts sever minds and sever worlds.

Why not try it out sometime?

The games upheld in court are known to be forced on the streets.

"Bad times have scientific value. These are occasions a good learner would not miss."
- *Ralph Waldo Emerson*

Being an author and engineer of *I R Physics*, and having been through a lot of bad times myself, I've been unfortunate enough to have discovered and then attempted to relay some national self-destructive trends that need to be fixed. And therein lays the potential for improvements, new advancements, legitimate discoveries and good opportunities.

"Our scientific power has outrun our Spiritual power. We have guided missiles and misguided men."
– *Martin Luther King, Jr.*

Here's an example of figuratively prescribing literal inferior destruction: What do you do when it's illegal not to follow a judicial supersuperior?
You accept it and follow.
But what do you do when you know by experience, legitimate experience that your superior cannot possibly have while having a job that's detached from reality and humans are stranded down in reality, that it's not only illegal to follow a judicial supersuperior but it's impossible as well?

You "*try*" (**Impossible)** [*SUFFER!*] to follow. (Enforced if need be.)

If you've been the literal victimized victim of figurative first-hand compulsive victimization I want to hear from you. Even if you followed their lead and self-destructed. And hopefully, we can enlighten impossible systems by gaming these systems that are gaming us. Inherently dissolving those systems who almost instinctively create to take advantage of, and inherently dissolve their own created helplessly dependents.

For those create dependence and hurt. Not independence and help.

Only We the People can and will unite to create independence and help. Not dependence and hurt.

Please join me in the Sound Proof LOOP of safety The uniting strengthening place for a Scientific Universe. Meant to unite fixing national self-destructing trends.

Therein lays the potential of a brand new world. A new world of engineering governments.

I'll now spend the rest of my days finally able to abide within higher standards, healing solutions, developing truth and/or incubating truth.

After all, what else can I do? Stay invisibly shallow too?

What's gamed in court;
is forced onto the streets.   339   *What's proven in PASS;*
                                                    is proven on the streets.

26. {PASS}^{2}

{PASS}^{2} – {Parents Against Satanic Standards} times {Parents Authorizing Scientific Standards} in the courtroom and beyond,{PASS}^{2} compulsively unauthorizes the old and competes with anew.

{PASS}^{2} legitimately competes with the exclusive group now severing in severance.

Why not practice and uphold uniting like they practice and uphold dividing?

Thanks to witting and willing Neglect our highest old final authority was under duress and/or enforced to be for hire.

And due to their own license scheme they had fixed themselves on top.

And the more crooked that they are on top the more profitable <u>and</u> the more politically favorable their dis-proportioning jobs become due to their own

What's gamed in court;
is forced onto the streets.   341   *What's proven in PASS;*
is proven on the streets.

fixed stages, their own fixed crooked
standards and their own fixed Severing in
Severance Principles (SSP.) The ideal
idol of manufacturing enmity. Leaving
legitimate parents, children and
institutions no choice but to follow
suit. With force if need be.

"*Justice*" and below was enforced to
be the most contrasting, the epitome of
contrary and the ultimate in trickery.

All of which automatically deviates
reality from fiction permanently and
perpetually more and more forever and
ever just like a well-oiled machine.

Thanks to unquestionable gross
negligence our highest enforced
"*authorities*" are the most corrupting,
the most expensive, and the most harmful.
Not to mention, the most needless.

{PASS}[2] naturally promotes 100% less
brainwashing and 100% more truth
developing.

100% of us were helplessly dependent
on being subjects to SSP (Severing in
Severance Principles) and their
uncorrectable, unconscious and even
compulsive Contrasting, Contrary and
Trickery Standards (CCTS.) If, by nothing
else, our licenses alone. If by anything
more, our reality.

Statistics show that 90% of all

What's gamed in court;
is forced onto the streets. 342 *What's proven in PASS;*
is proven on the streets.

runaway children are from divided homes. But reality would prove that 100% of those divided people grew up helplessly dependent on the exclusive group's SSP (Severing in Severance Principles) and CCTS (Contrasting, Contrary and Trickery Standards.)

SSP and CCTS are now known to not only destabilize psyches and destabilize worlds, but to actually sever psyches and sever worlds.

According to the US DHHS Bureau of the Census, 63% of youth suicides are from divided homes.

Reality on the other hand proves that 100% of those divided people were helplessly dependent on SSP and CCTS.

SSP and CCTS are now known to not only cause PBBA (Parent Blocking Bully-ism Abuse) but to literally be PBBA.

85% of children that exhibit behavioral disorders come from divided homes according to the Center for Disease Control.

Reality on the other hand enforces that 100% of those divided people are helplessly dependent on SSP, CCTS and PBBA.

Do you see a possible connection here? Or do you just feel the direct side effects unspeakably?

Fixing the most probable cause obviously fixes the most probable effects.

(Unless you prefer supporting the delusioning lands of make believe of course!)

You see, some of us don't get to be dads even if we wanted to. Once victims learn how to play the system just like the system makes them, then all bets are off and the straight and narrow have no chance or choice but to be crooked and play the system by its own rules just to compete.

Others enforce that it is this way.

Others neglect that it's this way.

Otherwise, they would only expose their own liability.

And they couldn't have that. Or else they'd have to accept some responsibility.

But 80% of rapists motivated with displaced anger come from divided homes according to *Criminal Justice and Behavior*, Vol. 14 p. 403-26.

100% of rapists were, are and will be

What's gamed in court;
is forced onto the streets. 344 *What's proven in PASS;*
is proven on the streets.

helplessly dependent on SSP, CCTS and
PBBA.
Talk about manufacturing criminals!

What's gamed in court;
is forced onto the streets.   345   *What's proven in PASS;*
is proven on the streets.

Are we figuratively helping or are some jobs literally "*Helping*" with force?

Are they "*civilizing*" or uncivilizing the world?

What's obvious about the obvious? How about the obvious?!

Children from divided homes are almost five times as likely to commit suicide. And 100% of those victimized victims were, are and will be dependent on being helplessly victimized.

Children from divided homes are almost seven times as likely to become teenage mothers. And 100% of those victimized victims were, are and will be dependent on being helplessly victimized.

Children from divided homes are almost twenty five times as likely to run away. And 100% of those victimized victims were, are and will be dependent on being helplessly victimized.

Children from divided homes are almost sixteen times as likely to have behavioral disorders. And 100% of those victimized victims were, are and will be dependent on being helplessly victimized.

What's gamed in court;
is forced onto the streets.   347   *What's proven in PASS;*
is proven on the streets.

Children from divided homes are almost seventy three times more likely to be killed. And 100% of those victimized victims were, are and will be dependent on being helplessly victimized.

Children from divided homes are almost eleven times as likely to commit rape. And 100% of those victimized victims were, are and will be dependent on being helplessly victimized.

What's the future? As is, scientifically, permanently and perpetually "*more*" and/or More of the same with force.

What's obvious, self-evident and/or self-provable is obvious, self-evident and/or self-provable.

Anyone can test this out for themselves.

Protecting SSP, CCTS and PBBA (inherently at the expense, the pain and the suffering of their victims) is the ultimate in Delusional Paradoxing (DP.)

DP (Delusional Paradoxing) is now known to Hypocrisize, Superhypocrisize, Systematically Euthanize, Systematically Kidnapped, and/or "*worse*" with force.

What's gamed in court;
is forced onto the streets.
348
What's proven in PASS;
is proven on the streets.

(See the book *Rocky Proxies,* by Certified American Aaron W. Wemple.)

If a pack of vicious dogs are known to maul unsuspecting little children why would anyone let the dogs enforce all of the rules?

{PASS}[2] is on the Order, cause and effects of The Upright USA Race and Family Matters Mission. With higher standards, healing solutions, reasoning towards understanding and incubating truth. It's soundproof.

Why not love uniting like others work so hard at dividing? {Or, I should say, compulsively *"uniting"* (**Dividing) [HIDING DIVIDING LIKE A MACHINE!]**}

Let us not likewise divide and conquer the Weegie Wedge. But let us uphold uniting at least level with and equal to the compulsively dividing, enmity manufacturing, Weegie Wedging in court inherently forced out into the streets.

Let us not fix national self-destructing trends, but rather AT least LET opportunities for healing to exist.

What's gamed in court;
is forced onto the streets.

What's proven in PASS;
is proven on the streets.

27. Free Gold with Free Glory! (Define 21st Century Freedom)

{By & for the Kingdom of God, of course.}

"Worthy is the Lamb, who was slain, to receive power and wealth and wisdom and strength and honor and glory and praise!"

I don't want money. Wanting money can be a trap worse than their traps.

I want the truth. And I want the truth to come out. The truth can be freeing more than our Founding Father's freeing.

And I want the truth hiders and binders to be held back. In the name of Love by and for but the LORD Jesus Christ I pray!

So, as long as it's in those respects any Constitutional Christian Parent has the Lord and I's permission to use the follow complaint to right some wrongs. To fix some broken systems and/or some broken superiors. Or to charge some broken supersystems and/or supersuperiors with Conspiracy.

Just don't ever believe in any court's (or its practitioners) authority more than you believe in the absolute authority of Love by and for but through Jesus Christ. Because only the later can and will shatter all other chains. Even invisible chains.

You may change the underlined parts of the following complaint as the Lord guides you to fit your needs if this is your calling. It's not for the light hearted. You own all over this place. It's ultimately serious.

It does not matter if a case wins or loses by a judge's decision. (Who is a fiction creating "*judge*" really anyway?!) It only matters if we see it through until the end.

This will help victims of SSP, CCTS and PBBA get the attention that they need just to survive.

It helps to collect evidence and witnesses along the way by standing up for the truth. In which your opponent(s)

will usually victimize you for it.
Because them *"gaming"* systems is routine
and automatic today.

When you find your abusive
competitor (usually a *"law"* School, *"law"*
System and/or a *"law"* Superior) then put
their name in place of the underlined
"St. Louis University" defendant on my
Civil Complaint template.

Usually the biggest Lever (bully)
weight is the easiest to correct.

But the goal to even fixing them
permanently and perpetually forever is to
win. Often times all that takes is just
seeing it through. Because given the
weight of their own pressures only the
truth will be squeezed out. And sometimes
all that it takes is just time and
intensity for a final result to sink in.
You have to be patient. You're waiting on
them to catch up. But you want to own
that final result.

And whether it's in the supersystem
or not is irrelevant. The truth will be
squeezed out. And that's the ultimate
goal. It will be easier together.

It's virtually impossible for most
people to truly see things from God's
perspective. We all have our own filters
blocking the view. Our own life
experiences and obvious distractions

What's gamed in court;
is forced onto the streets.   353   *What's proven in PASS:*
is proven on the streets.

easily get in the way simply by their presence alone.

But if you spend a lot of time in God's Word and away from all of the distractions of this world then you start to realize how different God's way is from the world's way.

The more that you learn about Jesus, the more that your problems dissolve.

In God's world it's always the little people who even have any potential to be lifted up. And even then it's not up to us. It will be to glorify God.

It's only the little people who can legitimately make a legitimate difference.

It has to be the little people who oppose giants by sticking to the truth regardless. Those are God's chosen children. Always has been and always will be. (I thank you Father that this seems good to you.)

That's true life. That's true light. That's true Word. That's the owner's manual.

Now, the path gets easier and easier over documented time and understood teaching as it gets clearer and clearer to see.

And that too is inevitable given light blockers are kept in check.

And today's no different. But it's time to get some light blockers in check. And there's now more than enough information to do it. With plenty of evidence available.

Most will probably accept it and move on. Like it's no big deal.

But those stuck in the old tight will have to stay stuck until the bitter end.

But that's no thing for a good soldier. Because we're in it to win it. And winning this is finishing this.

And why not capitalize on LOVE? Bringing us all into the true loop of life.

After all, LOVE is God. Who else cares about Him like we do? They can't.

They capitalize on hate. Dragging us all down into their absence of light.

It's time that we practice and uphold uniting at least equal to their practicing and upholding of dividing.

My family for example, was a one day one page $15 uniting license for us. And a 15 year two thousand page $150,000 dividing license for them.

Likewise for every other "*uniting*"

license, paper, statute, plastic, policy or practice that there is in America.

One piece of paper or plastic "*bait*" equals infinite corrupting, expense and human damages to us.

But infinite power <u>and</u> money for them dividing us under the fronts of "*uniting.*"

America, we have been hijacked.

When compliance to Rule, rules and rulers is impossible to follow, and enforced likewise, then what chance or choice do we have left but to just lay down and die?

In other words, follow the lead?

What's gamed in court;
is forced onto the streets.   356   *What's proven in PASS;*
is proven on the streets.

THIRD JUDICIAL CIRCUIT COURT OF ILLINOIS

Edwardsville, IL

[Your County (State Circuit) and/or Federal District court goes on top.]

Aaron W. Wemple (Your name here) (Plaintiff)

vs.

14-L-1138

St. Louis University (law school) (Defendant)

(The clerk puts

case number here.)

CIVIL COMPLAINT

NOW comes Aaron W. Wemple, Plaintiff pro se (representing one's self), to initiate this complaint, stating that:

1. The Plaintiff claims that the defendants are indoctrinating students, and therefore the real world beyond school, with Leverage and not Law as advertised;

2. The Plaintiff claims that the Defendants wittingly & willingly mislead students, student's parents, charity organizations, citizens, local, state, federal, and world officials alike for financial gain;

3. The Plaintiff believes that when more formal evidence is placed on one side of the scale then that increases the Leverage, not Law;

4. The Plaintiff believes that true Law is not leverageable, but absolute;

5. The Plaintiff claims that per his life long experience and scientifically indoctrinated research Leverage is impossibly being force fed as "*law;*"

6. The Plaintiff claims that true Law is teachable and does

What's gamed in court;
is forced onto the streets.   357   *What's proven in PASS;*
is proven on the streets.

not have to be force fed, flattery fed or trickery fed as something that it can never really be; And something that can never possibly stick;

7. The Plaintiff believes that the Defendant's promoting, teaching, indoctrinating, persuading and/or pressing that Leverage is somehow really "*law*" systematically Hypocrisizes victims;

8. The Plaintiff claims that having <u>University Physicists, Psychiatrists & Attorney's</u> on staff that the Defendants should know this;

9. The Plaintiff seeks <u>fifty million</u> dollars in compensatory damages on the grounds of Gross Neglect;

10. The Plaintiff seeks <u>two hundred million</u> dollars in punitive damages to exclusively offend systematic corrupting, defend systematic correcting, offend harming people & defend healing people by & for Human Authority;

11. For records the Plaintiff reminds this Court that Accountability & Neglect of Catastrophes are three State Statute violations easily "*law*;"

12. The plaintiff feels that the only thing more criminal than Leverage is hiding Leverage as something else;

13. The Plaintiff feels that the only thing more corrupt & more harmful than hiding Leverage as something else is hiding Leverage as "*law*;" Hiding Leverage as something that it can't be;

14. The Plaintiff feels that the only thing more corrupting & more assaulting than hiding Leverage as "*law*" is Neglecting hiding Leverage behind "*law*;"

15. The Plaintiff claims that <u>St. Louis University</u> has made millions of dollars unethically misleading millions of people causing irreparable systematic corrupting and irreparable

What's gamed in court;
is forced onto the streets.

What's proven in PASS;
is proven on the streets.

human damages.

     WHEREFORE, the Plaintiff prays that this court will hear this case in order to protect helpless, naive & unsuspecting young minds from being potentially Hypocrisized and/or worse. (Which must, according to *I R Physics*, perpetually increase the cause in size, duration, intensity & the mechanical defects likewise just to maintain the accused "*front*" until either implosion or explosion Transfiguration results.)

          Respectfully,

          _____

          <u>Aaron W. Wemple</u>, pro se
          (Your address here.)
          Team Clean Law

Operation *Flipped Vics*: Engineering Systems Upright after Dying from Systems Down-low

(Adjustments, copies, publishing, distribution & filing of this Complaint are permitted.)

What's gamed in court;
is forced onto the streets.
361
What's proven in PASS;
is proven on the streets.

What's gamed in court;
is forced onto the streets.

What's proven in PASS;
is proven on the streets.

THIRD JUDICIAL CIRCUIT COURT OF ILLINOIS

Edwardsville, IL

Aaron W. Wemple (Plaintiff)

vs.   No. 11-L-1138

St. Louis University, et. al. (Defendants)

AFFIDAVIT OF DAMAGES

SUPREME COURT RULE 222B

The undersigned being first duly sworn upon oath, deposes and states that he/she is a party to the above entitled cause of action seeking money damages or collection of tax and states that this cause of action does exceed $50,000.

_____

<u>Aaron W. Wemple</u>, pro se

(Your Address here)

Goals: Heal harming & promote healing,

Heal corrupting & promote correcting.

Sworn and subscribed before me

Date:_____

_____

Notary Public/Circuit Court Clerk

What's gamed in court;
is forced onto the streets.   363   *What's proven in PASS;*
is proven on the streets.

The Law Doctor

PROOF OF SERVICE

I certify that a copy of this Civil Complaint, Rule 222b & this Proof of Service was placed in a properly addressed sealed envelopes and placed in a post office box in the Edwardsville, Illinois post office on September 30, 2014.

<u>Aaron W. Wemple</u>, pro se

(Your address here.)

Associate: Clean Level Law Union

With higher standards & healing solutions.

Cc: <u>University President</u> (Address here.)

Questionable party: <u>Dean of Engineering</u> (Address here.)

Questionable party: <u>Psychiatric Dean</u> (Address here.)

Questionable party: <u>Chair in Law</u> (Address here.)

Et. Al. (means "and others" in English)

What's gamed in court;
is forced onto the streets.   365   *What's proven in PASS;*
is proven on the streets.

What's gamed in court;
is forced onto the streets.

What's proven in PASS;
is proven on the streets.

If you feel that it's on you to fix a system and/or a superior, to right a wrong, then stay calm, file the complaint, study my points, understand your opponents, and then just go through the motions that the court gives you.

The attention to details comes at the end. So that's where you're ready to express the climax of your case.

Ask for a trial in front of a jury because these cases are easy to prove. But hard to understand when pride's in the eye.

Ask for a speedy trial first because they will try to trick you out of your day in court.

And together we'll develop and/or incubate truth together.

If you're trying to get something out of the courts then you need to play along. That's what was always my problem. My issues where the courts themselves so I could not play along.

But if you're like me and you can't comply with courts then make your work public. Make your feelings known. Come together with those of a like mind. And that helps to enable change.

They have a bigger stage with like-minds in the media.

But we have a broader platform.

What's gamed in court;
is forced onto the streets.
367
What's proven in PASS;
is proven on the streets.

Theirs is fast and frivolous.
But ours is slow and stable.
They cannot legitimately beat us forever.

Anything that your opponent has mailed out under false pretenses is accusedly mail fraud. So you could try to report that and obtain additional evidence, witnesses and/or attention for your case and cause. Especially if it's grossly neglected.

Anything that your opponent has emailed out under false pretenses is accusedly internet fraud. So you could try to report that and obtain additional evidence, witness and/or attention for your case. Especially if it's grossly neglected.

Guilt or innocence is only up to a jury to decide. All others are tricksters.

Those taking reports have no legitimate decision. They are meant to report based on evidence and/or witnesses alone.

Prepare and mail out Affidavits like the one below. This is an easy way to obtain evidence and to see who your witnesses might be.

People are intimidated and so scared today that they don't want to stir up any trouble. That's the biggest obstacle to get over. So it's hard to find support in these areas.

Jesus (the way, truth and light) said that, "I did not come to bring peace, but a sword."
- *Matthew 10:34*

Exposing the truth, like showing the way with light, naturally opposes those who are stuck with the false. Who'd rather hide the light than expose their own error? So accepting forgiveness is on them just like it's on the rest of us.

Winners forgive.

The truth is the only thing that can even set them free is forgiveness. So you're helping them too no matter how much they hate it. It's for their own good to shine the light on them, regardless.

So shine it all over the world!

"It is not how much we have, but how much we enjoy, that makes happiness."
- *Charles Spurgeon*

What's gamed in court;
is forced onto the streets.   369   *What's proven in PASS;*
is proven on the streets.

TRUTH IN EDUCATION TRUE DEMOCRACY TRUTH IN JUSTICE AFFIDAVIT

(Evidence of one of Plaintiff's non-negligent social acts.)

Thank you for your time and consideration with this Affidavit to either help protect impressionable young minds or to help encourage impressionable young minds.

(Please circle either A1 or 1A next to the statement that you believe is true.)

A1 -   I think and/or know that <u>St. Louis University</u> *"law"* school is <u>indoctrinating</u> by & for hiding Leverage.

1A -   I think and/or know that <u>St. Louis University</u> *"law"* school is <u>indoctrinating</u> by & for revealing Law.

Thank you for your time and consideration serving your country in this most trying time. And for helping ensure that this world upholds the highest standards possible for all future generations. And for enlightening others so that healing solutions are not criminal and/or *"worse."*

Name:_____Date:_____

Signature:_____

Address:_____

Email:_____Phone:_____

What's gamed in court;
is forced onto the streets.   371   *What's proven in PASS;*
is proven on the streets.

Author of Human Authority,

_____

Aaron W. Wemple
(Your address here.)
Sound Proof Innovations -
Designing Systems Upright;
After Dying from Systems Down-Low;
Promote correcting, healing & saving;
Demote corrupting, hurting & wasting;
Upright USA Family Matters;
Higher Standards & Healing Solutions
Incubating Truth.

(Copies, distribution, publishing & ad lib are permitted.)

What's gamed in court;
is forced onto the streets.　373　*What's proven in PASS;*
is proven on the streets.

What's gamed in court;
is forced onto the streets.

What's proven in PASS;
is proven on the streets.

Knot Binder – The UQ (Ultimate Quagmire) "compromise."
The follow-up letter (about two weeks after suit is filed) to
cure mental cancer:

Aaron W. Wemple
Clean Law Union
September 6, 2014

St. Louis University (and others who may or may not be
culpable)
Office of the President
1 North Grand
St. Louis, MO 63103

Re. Madison County, IL civil case number 14-L-1138
complaining about possible "law" school mistake.

Dear St. Louis University President:

    I pray that this letter finds you well.

    I pray that you are beginning to understand
inherently suppressing systematic dynamics.

    Far too often in reality helplessly dependent people
are being wasted at our own expense.

What's gamed in court;
is forced onto the streets.   375   *What's proven in PASS;*
is proven on the streets.

Far too often jobs detached from reality intuitively hide literal leverage behind figurative "law" enabling themselves without even conscious ability of their own severed victims.

I know the routine. This is how innocent people go to prison. This is how dictating jobs impulsively take advantage of their own helplessly dependent victims. Something has to change.

Neglecting the obvious, self-evident and/or self-proving only forces the hands of the abused. So why not resolve the UQ so that we are then able to properly manage it & the inherent changes to come?

I protect people at my own expense. Nothing else matters. Jobs are replaceable. People are not as lucky. I've suffered from this issue. And studied the results first-hand my entire life.

I've been the permanent and perpetual victimized victim helplessly dependent on being dictated against by self-protecting, counter-intuitive, inherently bullyism jobs. As have my children. The damage is done. It's unconscionable. It's unaccountable. And it's irreparable. Save for the Light of Jesus Christ.

I've witnessed people die due to this compulsive abuse

What's gamed in court;
is forced onto the streets.   376   *What's proven in PASS;*
is proven on the streets.

and due to the compulsive neglect of this abuse. It's instinctive by nature. It's not intentional. But I've witnessed children kill themselves because they were legally tricked into not knowing, but left feeling the burdening pains permanently and perpetually forever. Pain and suffering proportional to the intensity "required" to keep victims from knowing in order to protect job liability issues. It figuratively and/or literally gags you. A total waste. A total waste to suppress victims bolstering jobs.

Not knowing is the bully here. Neglect is a close accomplice. The jury is still out as far as "Transparency." So why not help it out? After all, isn't enlightenment what the university is all about? So why intellectually divide when you could easily & more beneficially **intellectually unite**? That seems right.

Now, I'm not saying that St. Louis University is causing intellectual blindness, I'm just asking by the same terms that you teach if St. Louis University will cooperate with our independent study of experienced subjects to scientifically prove and/or scientifically disprove whether:
#1 - If "law" school is really leverage school;
#2 - If "law" school is really "hiding" leverage school; and
#3 – is it safe?

Please help students know what they're buying into. Please help students know if "lawyers" really manage leverage. And if people are ever really able to know the truth? And should people ever know the truth? And if absolute Bipolarism in court should ever quite possibly impossibly be labeled "law?" And if so then is this counter-productive? And should it be productive instead? And what does it do to impressionable young minds to believe that permanent & perpetual Bipolarism is law? And does it hurt them to follow it? And what does this do to impressed scientific minds who already know and understand real Law? Thus, never being able to accept intellectual dividing with force as somehow magically being inherently degraded as "law?" And are we degrading and/or destroying ourselves?

I can attest to the later (permanent & perpetual victimization compulsively simply for knowing.) 296 times victimized so far. It's a life of Hell (figuratively and/or literally.) And needlessly so I might add.

And if it is permanent & perpetual Bipolarism then is it safe for judges to be constantly exposed to this? Or are we putting them at risk?

Can we degrade & destroy our enemies abroad

What's gamed in court;
is forced onto the streets.   378   *What's proven in PASS;*
is proven on the streets.

without learning to degrade & destroy at home?

And if it is all manifesting permanent & perpetual Bipolarism into reality then would it be safer to fix the cause rather than to keep cleaning up all of the messes from it?

And if the "law" is either accept figurative Bipolarism or else you will feel literal Bipolarism "hidden" behind something else then where does this lead us as a nation? And if we follow it too long then where will it take us individually? I can attest it's a death sentence. And are there other options available?

And if we are "hiding" forcing people Bipolar then maybe "helping" them be psychotic and/or sociopathic would keep "protecting" the accused mistake?

Does "shooting from the hip" backfire down in reality? And if so would it be more humane to show us the marks up front on all the smart students? And is it safe promoting that the marks are on the front but later finding out only the harder way and/or the harder ways that they are really on our backs after all? And is UQ sane, safe and civilizing "saying" one thing on the front side of the scale but then to "do" another thing on the other back side of the scale?

So, I'm not saying that St. Louis University is causing

confusion, but you may be neglecting the cause of disorder by promoting that it's the highest "law" in the land that helplessly dependent victims have to quite possibly impossibly believe or else we literally go to jail and/or "worse" for. You may be teaching students to force us to eat this Ultimate Quagmire (UQ.) But it may not be possible to eat. In fact, it may be intellectually poisonous to eat. And if anyone other than your "highest" students say that it's poisonous to eat, then, well, jobs will be Ordered to force feed it to us. Do you see the Hell Hole inherently created here? Figuratively "die" and/or literally die. Figuratively "kill" and/or literally kill.

We're owed transparency, not inherently Hell. We're owed Rights, not suppression. We're owed process, not survival of the staged to be "fittest."

We're owed Democracy, not Hyopocrisy.

I'm proposing a Bill called the Law of Transparency. An Illinois State Statute and United States Act promoting people know that they have to be subject to Bar members and/or Hell. Bar members and/or Hell that St. Louis University accusedly "enlightens." Thus, enabling the Scientific Law of Leveraging Order to finally be legal (20 years after compulsively systematically murderizing its

What's gamed in court;
is forced onto the streets.   380   *What's proven in PASS;*
is proven on the streets.

discovery.)

Your students not only have the right to know, but they absolutely need to know just to protect themselves and their children. What if "law" school is actually the furthest thing from Law that there is?

I know that it would be easier and self-serving to hold us captive without complying with light, but why not pursue knowledge while serving your student's best interests instead? Please help the abused.

Let us find out if we're really living in an impossible "fantasy" land can we please? I am begging you. For the sake of our children and grandchildren and your students alike. Please help us know.

Why not let the helplessly dependent people see? Why protect labels instead of students, victims and the People?

Aaron W. Wemple - Intellectologist
The Sound Proof Safety Firm
"*Systems, Standards and/or Superiors of the Light.*"
"*Test the read. Know the light. Be the switch.*"
Why not see to protect yourself?
Why not see to fight for yourself?
Why not see to protect your children?

What's gamed in court;
is forced onto the streets.   381   *What's proven in PASS;*
is proven on the streets.

Why not know to know you're Right?
Maybe there's an ulterior motive that we need to iron out?
Maybe delusioning has more rights than students, victims &
People without a doubt?!

I know that switching lights on hurts when you're
vested in switching lights off. But I can't ignore this. I can't
let students be harmed and watch victims suffer for this UQ.
Especially since engineers taught me to know better. I'm
tired of seeing the self-sabotaging games that people have to
play just to fit in compliance with "Lights Off" systems,
standards and/or superiors.

The Law of Leveraging Disorder is figurative "compliance literally impossible to defy. Defined as the 21st Century
Crucifixion.

Scientific Trials (with Spot Trials Live) will inherently
enlighten and end all of this needless nonsense now being
accusedly taught. (Watch for my theoretical physics book
entitled "I R Physics" on Amazon to learn more about
enlightenment.)
(Sound Proof Safety Systems - Protection from systems,

What's gamed in court;
is forced onto the streets.   382   *What's proven in PASS;*
is proven on the streets.

standards and/or superiors that inherently keep and/or turn light off.)

(Sound Proof Safety Standards – Earning a new way to legalize systems, standards and/or superiors that inherently keep and/or turn light on.)

(Sound Proof Safety Superiors - Protecting helplessly dependent people at our own expense instead of wasting helplessly dependent people at their own expense.)

The Law of Leveraging Order is figurative words literally possible to follow. Defined as 21st Century Freedom.

Our Race is to discover, our mission is to unite relief from the inherently dividing pain & suffering caused from shoring up enmity due to the idle of enmity being upheld.

Because why permanently & perpetually divide when we are the United States of America?! Let's race mission?!

What's gamed in court;
is forced onto the streets.   383   What's proven in PASS;
is proven on the streets.

PROOF OF SERVICE

I certify that a copy of this letter to St. Louis University President dated September 6, 2014 and this Proof of Service were placed in properly addressed sealed envelopes and placed in a mailbox at the Edwardsville, IL Post Office on September 8, 2014.

Respectfully,

Aaron W. Wemple

The Scientific Sound Proof Safety Task Force,

Freedom from Crucifixions,

With higher standards & healing solutions,

Heal harming & promote healing,

Heal corrupting & promote correcting,

Heal wasting & promote saving.

www.CleanLawUnion.com

What's gamed in court;
is forced onto the streets.   385   *What's proven in PASS;*
is proven on the streets.

Love 2 win.

"Happy Birthday My Dear Sons" (If I could only know where you are.)

Some jobs are instinctive;
    Keep dad's authority & children able to follow it apart;
Some jobs work full-time;
    Keeping Founding Father's & children knowing about
their inheritance apart;

Bullyism is as bullyism does;
    Roses to victim's mothers;
Keeps 'em laughing from above.

How'd a judge steal the name of my child without my
knowledge?
    How'd a judge rob the terms of our inheritance
without our knowing?
"Happy Birthday my dear sons;"
    (I guess your gifts are lack of knowledge and never
really knowing.)

Enemy-ism is as Enemy-ism does;
    Roses to victim's mothers;
Keeps 'em laughing from above.

God's justice is instinctive;
    Just unite parents and children together;
God's children work full-time;
    Enlightening "dividing" keeping us in line with our inheritance.

Christ-ism is as Christ-ism done;
    Roses to bullies fathers;
Keeps God smiling up above.

America was meant to be instinctive;
    Just unite & don't divide;
Inherent jobs work full-time;
    Keeping enmity held up high;

"Study-ism" is as "study-ism" does;
    Truth to systems masters;
Keeps eyes looking above.

What's gamed in court;
is forced onto the streets.　389　*What's proven in PASS:*
is proven on the streets.

What's gamed in court;
is forced onto the streets.

What's proven in PASS;
is proven on the streets.

Abbreviations

3-CCDD: Three Complex Concurrent with Divisional Dimensions

3CUCD: Compulsively Uniting Complex Dividing (a.k.a. Weegie Wedging paradigm scheme)

APD: Abusive Power Disordered

CCD: Concurrent Complex Dimensions

CCTS: Contrasting, Contrary & Trickery Standards

CD-VD: Compulsively Dividing - Vices Device

CIDVVD: Compulsively Intimidating Dividing Vices and/or Vises Device

DDS: Duel Death Spiral

DLA: Disordering Leverage Association

HVVE: Helpless Victimized Victim Effect

JOP: Judicial Operating Procedure

LLD: Law of Leverage Disordered

LLO: Law of Leverage Order

MMD: Motor of Mass Destruction

SSP: Severing in Severance Principles

STD: Static-Transferring Dynamics

UJE: Ultimate Judicial Enigma

UQ: Ultimate Quagmire

WSA: World Star Association

    The Law Doctor's Prescription for 2015: Sound Proof presents "Peace" Summits in various cities, counties, states, etc. Upright USA & Family Matters will unite to dissolve dividing.
    The Law Doctor's Prescription for 2020: Wemple's Antivirus in Governing Policies & Practices Software. Upright USA & Family Matters will unite to dissolve dividing.
    The Law Doctor's Prescription for 2025: Dump the Weegie Wedge. The Upright USA Race with Family Matters Mission will unite to dissolve dividing.

That's Sound Proof!
Forgive & live.

What's gamed in court;
is forced onto the streets.   392   *What's proven in PASS;*
is proven on the streets.

Acknowledgments

Relief of burdens courtesy of Jesus Christ.

Documenting relief from burdens courtesy of Jesus' disciples.

Sharing documented relief from life's inherent burdens courtesy of Jesus followers.

Constitutional rule courtesy of Founding parents.

Deep gratitude of constitutional rule courtesy of Bar Associations members.

Cover text courtesy of cooltext.com

Cover seal courtesy of Say-it.com

Back cover picture - Visions by Carol

Photo edits courtesy of ipiccy.com

Word Processor courtesy of Open Office

Quotes from Dictionary.com & Brainy-quote.com

What's gamed in court;
is forced onto the streets.   393   *What's proven in PASS;*
is proven on the streets.

PAS (Parental Alienation Syndrome) by Author Linda Gottlieb.

And for more information about being or becoming a licensed author, a Certified American, a Certified Christian, a Sanctified Speaker, or any combination of the above please visit The Sound Proof Safety Firm.

Together uniting strengthening We the People are now the World Star Association. Children by & for the Upright USA Race Family Matters Mission.

Together, we win & we succeed.

Other books by Aaron W. Wemple:

  Old School Pet Care,
  American Pros,
  The New Scientific Citation Standards,
  I R Physics

Now informed uniting may be equal to informed dividing.

After all, isn't that what we're all all about?

(Maybe that's why dividing as an institution was so hard to see? Or, maybe it was because it was impossible to "*see*" or See!? before now? Please let enmity no longer judge People and/or Professions.)

BELIEVE JESUS.

What's gamed in court;
is forced onto the streets.

What's proven in PASS;
is proven on the streets.

Own True Love,

and own True life.

Love 2 win,

2 win Love.

What's gamed in court;
is forced onto the streets.
401
What's proven in PASS;
is proven on the streets.

www.ingramcontent.com/pod-product-compliance
Lightning Source LLC
Chambersburg PA
CBHW060834280326
41934CB00007B/774